Family Matters

Edited by Angela Fairbrace

forwardpress

First published in Great Britain in 2008 by:
Forward Press Ltd.
Remus House
Coltsfoot Drive
Peterborough
PE2 9JX
Telephone: 01733 890099
Website: www.forwardpress.co.uk

All Rights Reserved

© *Copyright Contributors 2008*

SB ISBN 978-1 84602 069 8

Foreword

Although we are a nation of poets we are accused of not reading poetry, or buying poetry books. After many years of listening to the incessant gripes of poetry publishers, I can only assume that the books they publish, in general, are books that most people do not want to read.

Poetry should not be obscure, introverted, and as cryptic as a crossword puzzle: it is the poet's duty to reach out and embrace the world.

The world owes the poet nothing and we should not be expected to dig and delve into a rambling discourse searching for some inner meaning.

The reason we write poetry (and almost all of us do) is because we want to communicate: an ideal; an idea; or a specific feeling. Poetry is as essential in communication, as a letter; a radio; a telephone, and the main criterion for selecting the poems in this anthology is very simple: they communicate.

Contents

Upon Leaving Home	Claire Tupholme	1
For You Dear Mum	Don Woods	2
Her Dad	Alline C Yap-Morris	3
Daddy	Vivienne Vale	4
No Such Thing	Laura Brocklebank	6
Dad	Christine Naylor	7
Thank You My Father	P K Janaky	8
Dad	Mary Woolvin	10
Missing You Today (Mother's Day)	Linda Casey	11
Happy Mother's Day	Leah Vernon	12
Mother's Day	Deborah Storey	13
My Mum	Rebecca Spencer	14
Mother	Elizabeth Slater Hale	15
My Mom, And God-Daughter Pamela's Auntie Dort	Jackie Adams	16
Revived	Susan Mullinger	17
Mothers	Donna Salisbury	18
Past And Present	Terry Daley	19
My Mother	Ndidi Ubogu	20
Mother Of The Mourning	Annie Pollock (12)	21
My Mother	Jenny Parker	22
Cherished Thoughts	Josephine Foreman	23
Finale	Laurence D E Calvert	24
Eighty-Six - Who's Counting?	Charles Keeble	25
The Robin	Brian Hurll	26
The Door Was Always Open	Denise Delaney	27
For My Mum, The Best In The World	Julie Marie Laura Shearing	28
My Precious Mum	Amy Kirk	29
My Mother Years After	Liz Davies	30
Old Mother	Jackie Oung	31
Tribute To Mothers	Prabha Margaret Peters	32
My Mum And I	Muhammad Khurram Salim	33
Poem For Lydia	Thelma Glanville	34
A Mother's Hands	Kathleen Potter	35
Mother's Day	Jane McCarty	36
I Thought That We'd Be Close Again	Philippa Bower	37
Mother's Day	William Lacewell Jr	38

Mother's Day (An Appreciation)	Anthony McGeehan	39
Thanks	Karen Edis	40
Mum's Letter	Ray Ryan	41
Mother	Dorothy Healey	42
I Wrote This For My Mother	Rebecca Dobson	43
A Mother's Heart	Sidney Talbot	44
Mother's Anxiety	Professor Kalyan Ray	45
My Mum	Chris Leith	46
Staring Bright: The Ages Of Woman	Carole Alexander	47
Darling Mum	Victorine Lejeune Stubbs	48
I Used To Watch You	Steve Kettlewell	49
Poem For Mum	Jon Elkon	50
Our Mother's Love	Glenwyn Peter Evans	51
My Mother - A Tribute	Beverley Harknett	52
My Time Over Again	John Bennetts	53
In Her Eyes	Rita Bridgman	54
Who Would Be A Mother?	Pauline Pickin	55
New Start	Carol Ponting	56
Cuddles	John Clarke	58
Stuck In The Middle	Eunice Ogunkoya	59
Eighty Years	George Coombs	60
Mother's Day	Frances Gibson	61
Lovely In Red	Amanda Houghton	62
Mother	Michelle Crozier	63
Mums Eh?	Andy Wheeler	64
Mums	Sophie Greig	66
Mum	Anne Sackey	67
For My Mother	Roland Gurney	68
My Lost Mum	Patricia Dawson	69
A Mother's Love	Vere Collins	70
My Hardworking Mother	Alan Hattersley	71
My Mum	Joy Toms	72
A Mother's Wish . . .	Robert Hessey	73
Mum	Angela Cole	74
Mothers	Alan Pow	75
Mum	Sheila Waller	76
An Angel	Gerard Jones	77
Frances Mary	Doreen Reeves	78
Mother	Diana Daley	79
Mums	Carolie Cole Pemberton	80
Dear Mum	Gary Murphy	81

A Mother's Love	Valerie Ovais	82
My Mum Was Always There	Corin Jasmine Dienes	83
My Mother Taught Me The Meaning Of Words	David Constable	84
Kissing Roses	Tina Molli	85
This Illustration : A Study In Desolation	Alan Knott	86
Pretty Girl	Julia Holden	87
Steve	Marina Reeves	88
Dannielle	Janet Granger	89
For Jake - Born Prematurely	Joanne Burns	90
Daughter . . . Lisa-Marie	Marie McCarthy	91
She Is There For Me	Gwyneth Scott	92
The Last Picture Show	Nigel Astell	93
Our Dearest Mother	Edna Adams	94
Welcome	Patricia Ammundsen	95
Forty Years On	Sheila Allen	96
Blessed Child	Shelagh Clare James	97
To My Dad	Farina May Jenkins	98
Your Dad	Joanne Jervis	99
My Daughter	Gilly Jones	100
My Son	Joyce Jones	101
Family History	Gwen Joselin	102
Gift Of Love	Shirley Allen	103
Special One	Jean Adam	104
To Holly	Dorothy Athorn	105
Sweet Music	April Dickinson-Owen	106
Ella And Freddie	Elaine Day	107
Luke	Gillian D'Arcy	108
Jack	Mary Daines	109
Baby It's You	Keith Powell	110
Mother	Janet Jannaway	111
Our Shirley's Birthday . . .	J Fred Jackson	112
I'd Like To Say	Margaret McGinty	113
For A Loving Mum	Rachelle Arlin Credo	114
My Little Sister	Ruth Berry	115
For The Loss Of A Mother	Christine Collins	116
A Prayer Will Help	Anne Churchward	117
A New Awakening	Laura Clarke	118
A Word	Kevin Clemo	119
Happy Times With Dad	Mavis Catlow	120
A Letter To My Dad	David J Hall	121

Sister She	Kiranjit Kaur Rana	122
For My Father	Elsie Hamilton	123
My Dad	Jennifer Collins	124
A Daughter	Tess McHugh	125
Julian	L J Roche	126
God Bless You This Mother's Day	Christopher R Slater	127
Olivia	Daisy Adams	128
My Little Poppet Skye	Joy Westmoreland	129
Clive	Valma June Streatfield	130
The Entranced Lovers	Joana Efua Sam-Avor	131
For Sam And Becky	Ruth Wright	132
October Sun	Bryony Freeman	133
The Young Musicians	Freda Grieve	134
My Grandson	V N King	135
Baby It's You!	Graham Watkins	136
Poem For Little Liam	Margaret Rose Harris	137
My Loved Ones	Carl Fricker	138
Apple Of Their Eye	J Millington	139
Adoption's The Option	Hazel J Palmer	140
My Son Got Married Last Week!	Margaret Rowe	141
In Remembrance Of Mum And Dad	James Ayrey	142
Loved Ones	Rosalind Ann Webb	143
Maltese Baby	Steve Glason	144
The First Grandchild	R D Hiscoke	145
Nature's Gift	Mavis Johnson	146
Our Firstborn	Daphne Fryer	147
Baby Love	A A Trick	148
Beau - My Great Grandson	Hazel Brydon	149
A Tiny Baby	David Sheasby	150
Another Generation	Janet Cavill	151
My Girl	Olive Young	152
Curtis, Aged Seven	Kathy Johnson	153
A Bond Of Love	Kathleen Webb	154
Her First Snowman	C M Creedon	155
Unfathered In The Packed Street	Rizwan Saeed Ahmed	156
Anniversary Sonnet For My Father	Edmund Saint George Mooney	157
At Seventy-Two	Geoffrey Speechly	158
Dear Dad	Linda Bevan	159

The Last Post	Debbie Nobbs	160
Being A Dad (This Is Totally True)	Barry Ryan	161
A Poem For Dad	Alexis Jarrett	162
Too Proud	Catherine Armstrong	163
Things My Father Taught Me	Iris Williams	164
My Family	Ellen Lock	165
My Lovely Dad	Kim Thompson	166
My Dear Dad	Patricia Marland	167
My Dad	Jean Martin-Doyle	168
To My Father	Rosemary Benzing	169
I Never Had A Dad	Helen E Langstone	170
Roundabout Of Life	Sheila Walters	171
Daddy Observed	Louie Carr	172
Father	Teresa Webster	173
The Daddy Dance	Joy Kelly	174
The Legend Of The Heroes	Stuart Adams	175
My Dad - Captain Of Love	Barbara Goode	176
Thank You Mum	David Cooke	177
Where Have You Gone?	Thésie Jenkinson	178

The Poems

October 2008.

To my dear friend Sue.
With love and respect,
Pat. x

Upon Leaving Home
(For Mum and Dad - because a simple 'thank you' is not enough)

If I looked up the words 'generosity'
And 'selflessness' in a dictionary
Instead of the normal black and white text
A picture of you two there would be

If I asked the glorious sun to shine
On people who've continuously shown me love
You would always bask in the idyllic warmth
Of the rays of light from up above

If I asked the refreshing rain to fall
In honour of the kindness and support you show
Even the driest rivers would burst their banks
And their waters overflow

If a musician was asked to write music
To show how special you are to me
The crowd would hear the orchestra
Playing a wondrous symphony

If I asked a sculptor to create
A monument to a happy home
The visitors to the gallery would see
The image of this house carved from stone

If you asked me to take all my memories
The ones I have of growing up here
And told me to give one to every scared person
Then no one would live in fear

If I asked for a song to be sung in thanks
You would wake to a dawn chorus from the birds
If you asked me to say how grateful I am
There simply wouldn't be enough words.

Claire Tupholme

For You Dear Mum

For you dear Mum a message
To show how much I care
For each morning as I greet the day
I know that you are there
Although this life has blessed me
With a family of my own
I still feel I'm your baby
Although I am full-grown.

Through the years you raised and cared for me
And etched your love deep in my heart
For you knew one day would come a time
When my own love I would impart
As I do to my own family
But don't forget dear Mum
The love you gave will stay with me
From now till Kingdom come.

Don Woods

Her Dad

My dearest daughter she needs her dad
Who can see the good in her, correct the bad
Who can be there when she grazes her knee
Can show her things that she should see
Can guide her through those turbulent years
Can be there to wipe away those tears
And tell her when she is wrong
But guide her, make her strong
Who can praise her when she gets top marks
And maybe, sometime, take her to the park
Who can be that true and understanding friend
To support her through the current trend.

Alline C Yap-Morris

Daddy

You were the one to whom I ran and sat me on your knee
The one to wipe away my tears, to hug and comfort me
Your gentle eyes that filled with tears whenever I was upset
And always reassured me and told me not to fret.

On school days, up at seven, my breakfast all prepared,
You saw me off to school; to me, no one could compare.
At bedtime always finding time to take me up the stairs
Staying by my side until I'd said my prayers.

Saturdays spent at the allotment, where you worked to tend our needs,
I'd help you in your vegetable patch to help dig out the weeds.
You'd feed the chicks, the ducks and pigs; never classing this
                                                            as chores
For, after working down the mines each day, you enjoyed
                                                            the time outdoors.

Every Sunday morning, to my grandmother's we would go.
We'd walk, my hand in yours, until we'd reach her door.
You were so much like your 'Mum', so gentle and so kind,
I felt so very fortunate; a finer Dad I'd never find.

In summertime we loved our walks, o'er hills quite near our home,
With Mammy and our dear pet, the mountains we would roam
The hours spent reminiscing of when you were a boy
And the love you had for horses, which gave you so much joy

You always were so strong and worked so hard back then
For working in the colliery turned young lads into men.
Then came the pit disaster; an explosion underground.
Lives were *lost* that day and the loss was so *profound*.

You never returned to the colliery again; they had to 'close it down'
So you worked the latter years in a factory downtown.
You missed the camaraderie, it was obvious to tell
And, after several years of working there, you became unwell.

Such special times we spent, together, you and I.
You always used to say I was 'the apple of your eye'.
Alas, being a coal miner took its toll upon your health,
Nothing could be done to help you . . . no amount of wealth.

Our great love for each other was soon put to the test.
For you were taken from me; twas time for you to rest.
Oh, how I *missed* you Dad; my world just fell apart.
And nothing could ease the aching in my heart.

But I've so *many* happy memories of how good you were to me
And I *know* that you are always looking over me
Now you are safe and well in a world that's free from pain
And sometime, in the future, we'll be *together* once again.

Vivienne Vale

No Such Thing

My father -
I cannot look him in the eyes anymore
How can I hide
The plaintive note in my voice?
The man who was
A god to me
In past times, he is now
My biggest disappointment.

I wish these walls
Would record my thoughts
Then I
Could lock my father
In this room
Let the bricks
Scream my feelings at him
Doing the dirty work
For me.
I hate him for
Leaving, for
Teaching me to
Run from good things and instead
Live life on quick fixes.

I also hate him because
I am confused, and
Somewhere
Love clouds the mixture
That hurts the most of all.

Laura Brocklebank

Dad

(In memory of George Arthur Bowdler Morris 1901 to 1976)

Dad - when I think of you, what do I see?
I believe I see a small part of me
Outwardly you seemed strong and tough
I was told your childhood was pretty rough
Around the streets you would often roam
To wait outside pubs till parents came home
And then I discovered a few weeks ago
That your natural father you did not know
But a child cannot be blamed for reasons of its birth
And circumstances do not change that child's worth
Now many other things have become more clear -
I knew your sister Beattie, who you held dear
But you had brothers that I never met
Though I may find out about them yet.
Too young for the first war though you gave it a go
And were turned away, the answer was no!
You went on to join the army as a young lad
And experienced many things, both good and bad
Too old in the second war to serve away
So on the anti-aircraft guns you had to stay
I don't think a third child was really in the plan
But I was born in the war to become part of the clan.
For much of my life you worked away from home
To give us the good things you'd never known
I wish you had known my daughter, Claire
You would have had a love of gardening to share
But sadly this was not meant to be so
Yet you would have loved her, this I know.
One day soon I will search your family tree
To try to find out what made me - me!

Christine Naylor

Thank You My Father

The only hours I live are the hours when,
I am absorbed by beauty, truth and wisdom,
That you have taught me to see in nature,
Watching the leaves fall and the flowers bloom,
The exquisite taste of solitary freedom,
Merging into a reverie of suspended thoughts,
Where your kind, calm face emerges within,
Thank you my father for just being there.

I wipe a teardrop at the thought of separation,
I hurry to do things that may make you happy,
I sit close to you reading your favourite books,
And feel fulfilled to receive the light wisdom,
Radiating from your tired, bright eyes,
You taught me to reclaim large areas of peace,
Rich with joy within me in a cruel world,
Thank you my father for the wisdom you gave.

Psychic disorders of the relations outside,
Cut through my heart, leaving deep wounds,
A mental, physical wreck, I came to you,
Seeking some comfort I lay down in your bed,
And nestled into your soft warm pillow,
Fragrant with sandal paste and the sacred ash you wear,
I felt your presence close, whispering in my ears,
Thank you my father for soothing my tortured mind.

Stroking my burning forehead with infinite kindness,
Through silent communion you imparted wisdom,
The teacher eternal taught me the truth,
Silence is the poise of mental balance,
The fruits of silence are true courage,
Dignity of character and true reverence,
Quite unshaken by the storms of existence,
Thank you my father, for relieving my pain.

The sacred silence of the morning sun,
The sweet summer earth and birds on the bough,
Make me rediscover the world of which,
I have the happiness of being a part,
The joy of wisdom that flows from you,
Has given me eyes to see me in all beings,
And to love everything as I love myself,
Thank you my father, the dispeller of my darkness.

Now your face so tired, with lines of wisdom,
I will not grieve when you depart to join my mother,
Birth and death and life between, is ordained by God,
You shall go with joy, your duties well-fulfilled,
To the Kingdom of God deserved by elevated souls,
I shall stand cheerful for I will join you soon,
When my cup of life too is full to the brim,
Thank you a thousand times for being our father.

P K Janaky

Dad

Father, dear Father
Every day is a blessing
My forehead you kiss
My face always caressing
You walk my walk
My hand in yours
You tread my steps
Sometimes two back
Sometimes you ponder
Sometimes you pause
Whatever I do in life
You're always there behind me
Whenever I come to talk to you
You listen with an open heart
You're always giving
You astound me
You are my bridge
Forever I will always walk
Some days are happy
Some days are dark
You're always there Dad to guide me
Whenever I do wrong, you're never mad
I love you so much
For loving me
My caring, wonderful
Loving Dad.

Mary Woolvin

Missing You Today (Mother's Day)

I miss you Mum
More than words can say
You are no longer here
For us to celebrate this Mother's Day
So the only thing
That I can do
Is to write
How much I love you
You were my mum
And also my friend
So these words to you
I do send
I miss you Mum every day
You were the best
You did so much for everyone
So you deserve to rest
I'll never forget your smiling face
Or the things you used to say
I just wish that you were still here today
So we could celebrate Mother's Day.

Linda Casey

Happy Mother's Day

Mother's Day has come around once more
I know you've heard these words before
You are so special, I just wanted to say
I love you more with each passing day
You are my mother, so loving and kind
If I go round the world I could never find
A mother so gentle and wonderful as you
Because no way on this Earth could there be two
I'm so very lucky to have you as my mum
You're there if I need you, you're also my chum
You're so very special they named a day after you
And you truly deserve it, you really do
No one is more treasured than you are today
I wish you much happiness and I just wanted to say
This is the only way that I can thank you
By putting into words how much I love you.

Leah Vernon

Mother's Day

Mother's Day
Brings me near
For the sound of your voice I can still hear

You're so special
That I'll say
Because we all love you on this very special day

So I know
I must not worry
No I must not weep

But it's hard to go on without you
And I know you love us all
The tears I shed
Are because I'm missing you

But to the Lord
I do pray
So I can thank you
On this, today, a special
Mother's Day.

Deborah Storey

My Mum

When she's stressed
She doesn't complain
But when she's tired
She's just the same

She cooks and cleans
All just for me
She makes me breakfast
Dinner and tea.

Rebecca Spencer

Mother

Sitting in the firelight
Lost in the flickering flame
I search the part that is my soul
And there I see your name

God placed me in your tender care
So my path was strong and sure
He knew you had the kind of love
That always would endure

What words can hope to ever describe
The essence that is Mother
How life itself depends upon
A love unlike no other

A love that will not fail us
As we journey through this life
That will shield us and sustain us
Against this world of strife

As women pass down the gift of life
From one unto the other
United in the miracle
That turns us into Mother.

Elizabeth Slater Hale

My Mom, And God-Daughter Pamela's Auntie Dort

My beloved mother,
If only you could hold my hand
As you did many a yesterday.

Those first four years when I couldn't walk
I cried and screamed but couldn't talk
Hospital doctors gave up -
You, Mom, persevered
For which you are revered.

Often, I caused you despair
The family helped you.
What a day,
You turned your head for just a few seconds,
'Where's my baby?'
Unaided, I was climbing the stairs!

Poor, we were, but a piano ours
For many hours
On your lap, Mom, I sat,
Your hands guiding my fingers across the keys,
No response from me, somewhere in my own world . . .
Then, *bang!* The lowest musical note -
Something in me awoke!

My childhood you gave to me
Days of doll and pram, hopscotch square,
Paints and books and skipping ropes
In the park on swings and slide,
Day trips, holidays, seaside, fairground rides and Elvis.

The 11+ I failed - But 'I'm in the top class Mom!'
Oh! your pride . . .
How soon time goes by to the tragic night of winter, moon and stars
My mother's life lost to the driver of a car.

Jackie Adams

Revived

Last week I thought that you were looking great
Buds coming out in bloom, I counted eight
Standing sturdy in the warm summer sun
Next day, noted what rain and wind had done.

Overnight, branches were battered and bruised
You looked very sad, like you'd been abused
But now with dry weather spell you've revived
I'm glad Mum's memorial rose survived.

Susan Mullinger

Mothers

Mothers are a bunch of saints
With a million things to do
Washing, cooking, cleaning
And tying the occasional shoe
They do the ironing and the shopping
And soothe fears of the head
And hug you nice and tight
As they tuck you into bed
They make the beds and clean the floors
They have patience and loyalty true
Let's give thanks to mothers
Who do all the things they do!

Donna Salisbury

Past And Present

The youngest girl of a large Welsh family
Born and still living in the Rhondda Valley
She is the last of that family's members
The others have gone, but always remembered.
After the Grammar School she went into nursing
But not for long as she soon started courting
In South Wales she married a wonderful man
Settled down, enjoyed life as families can
She worked hard, making many sacrifices
For husband and children, she had no vices
Five children were raised in the best tradition
To teach them proper values was her mission
Loved by all her family and relatives
And every neighbour in the street where she lives
In her nineties now, she is always caring
In spite of her failing eyesight and hearing
I speak I'm sure, for my sisters and brother
A small tribute to a wonderful *Mother.*

Terry Daley

My Mother
(Dedicated to Mrs Jane Ubogu)

Many years ago still I remember
Like yesterday your beauty still glitters like an angel
As you were so you are
And tears fall down when your white hair becomes visible

You were as strong as a lioness; so brave like a bear
You were as loving as a dolphin; too gentle like a dove
You were a protector, a shield, an umbrella . . . and a mother

My mother! A phrase I love so much
Mother of sweet-smelling flowers
The one I long to embrace each minute
The one I pray for without ceasing
The one I am proud of always
And the one I will always look after

My mother! My happiness, my sight
You are the cause of my endless joy
And these words I will always share
Your smile is a smile of life
Your words are pearls of wisdom
Blessed is Anthony Ubogu
Blessed are your children.

When I was little still I remember
You wrapped me in your arms go gently
Like a hen does to her chicks
You chased the cold wind away and I was never thirsty.

So smile that joyful smile sweet mother
Because your children love you so much
Yesterday to this day you remain the same
Indeed; you are the sweetest mother in the whole wide world
I love you my sweet mother.

Ndidi Ubogu

Mother Of The Mourning

Slowly it creeps
Around every crack,
The cold-hearted feeling
That makes you never turn back.
The brightness has gone,
Just darkness and gloom,
There is nothing more
There is no more room.
Eventually it comes
The thing that you needed,
The thing that you wanted,
The thing that you pleaded.
A steady flow of tears
That fall from your eyes,
Like the thick falling rain
That falls from the skies.
You know it's OK
That the pain will go
But you wonder how long,
You wonder when so.
Slowly it creeps
Around every crack,
The cold-hearted feeling
That makes you never turn back.
You know that she's gone,
She was like no other.
You'll never forget her
As she, was your mother.

Annie Pollock (12)

My Mother

I lay my head upon my mother's breast
Instant comfort, instant rest
All your problems seem to fade away
As words of wisdom she does display
Understanding and loving passion
Is given out in every fashion
Then as the years roll slowly on
My mother needs me to depend upon
Ill health and age creeps slowly near
Then to the end of her good life I fear
No one will ever replace her grace
As in my heart I will never forget her face.

Jenny Parker

Cherished Thoughts

The years have quickly passed
Since you were gone
Cherished thoughts last
Filling my heart with song

I feel you are with me every day
As though we be never apart
Cherished thoughts filled of you in every way
Dear Mother so deep in my heart

A good life you gave the family
Encouraging us to seek the light shining above
Even in days of calamity
You made each day glow

With cherished thoughts as often as I can
I visit your resting place
Singing the song you often sang
To honour thee dear Mother with grace

I would like you to know
I have settled in a pleasant place
With cherished thoughts of you aglow
Keeps me every day embraced

Although by myself feel not alone
With feelings of you by my side
Reminiscing happy times where're we did roam
Making each day pleasantly glide

Until the day we be as one
Your happy photos surround me
When we shared moments of fun
Cherished thoughts filling me with glee.

Josephine Foreman

Finale

Those last few months
Stripped away her life
And dignity
As her rogue cancer ate
Into her body
And into her quality of faith
As she cried out to Christ
As if she were a long-lost child
And each time it seemed He
Failed to respond to her little voice
And yet in-between the heavy
Shelling of her physical agony
She once again found new beams
Of hope and strength as her days
Became shorter and autumn arrived
In mid-summer
As children's voices drowned out
Her deepest plunge into the chilled
Waters of finality.

Laurence D E Calvert

Eighty-Six - Who's Counting?

She doesn't get around as much as she did
In nautical terms it's the cut of her jib
But in earlier times this young Yorkshire girl
Moved with such grace she had boys in a whirl.

Even marriage and children didn't slow the lass down
While living in Hampstead she was all over town
Worked at the clinic in Finsbury you know
Where the snipping brought tears and only the bravest would go.

When retiring to Devon for the fresh air and garden
Would you believe it her joints start to harden
But the Telegraph crossword keeps her mind sharp and clear
Mum, keep using your stick and we'll see you next year.

Charles Keeble

The Robin

Ever since her mother died, my wife has had a hunch
That a robin in our garden is her spirit, come for lunch
This may seem rather strange, but wherever we make our home
This little bunch of joy won't leave us alone.
We recently moved, to spend our latter years
It was only two days before he reappeared
Even when you speak to him, he never flies away
He cocks his head and looks at us, we think he's here to stay.
I walked into my tool shed to put some things away
And now he's in there nesting, busy all the day.
I have had to cut an access hole so he can come and go
When I lock up the shed at night and he just seemed to know.
I hope it is Mum's spirit, she was really good to me
It may just be our fantasy, but we must wait and see
When she died we rushed to her, never got to say goodbye
So maybe she has taken flight and come to live nearby.

Brian Hurll

The Door Was Always Open

Two doors were always open, yet guarded from gate-crashing spies
I could see her door in my mind and mine she could see with her eyes
My insides preyed upon that door, waiting for her to know and flee
But her eyes weren't on her escape, they were waiting for me.
One door led to her escape, my door safe under barricade
Not informed they were connected, I obsessed over the game
                                             that she'd played -
Not expecting to be dragged out my door then outside motherly laid.

Ways say farewell at dips in the road,
Well-known, so some are home-made
Her door was always open
Unsure why she stayed - no logic, no practice, no trust
Waited and waited to be betrayed . . .

In hindsight it was the other door open, she would not let herself flee
I could never understand quite why but she always waited for me
Walls and fortifications guard not against the key through lies
She knew right where to find me
And the opening was just the right size.

The voice in the dark that lights with your mask
But actually takes in the deafening need
Wise man when the time draws near
Instinctive what to wave or feed
Glorious passion with warmth behind armour
So shiny, bright and strong
Guide on the journey from worlds unto worlds
Still with you when all's said and done
Knowing through sheer presence and love
This family is where you belong.

Denise Delaney

For My Mum, The Best In The World

I wish I could be with you today
There is so much I want to say
I love you and think you are a star
We share an inner warmth wherever we are.

I want to hug you too
And cook a special meal just for you
But today the distance is too far
For me to travel in the car.

Mum, happy Mother's Day
I wish I could be with you today.

Julie Marie Laura Shearing

My Precious Mum

Her eyes sparkled green
She lived life to the full
She was the best she could be
My precious mum.

She loved to laugh
Or even chat
She would cry when she needed
But laugh after that.

When her arms wrapped around you
You would never want her to let go
Her sweet smell lingered
My precious mum with a heart of gold
And a smile of silver.

Her short black hair was soft
Her touch so smooth
Her face as pretty as a flower
Her love growing and growing
For evermore.

When it came to the end
We were all there
To watch God take her
For his garden of flowers
My precious mum.

Amy Kirk

My Mother Years After

I think of her now, years after,
How she would love to see us grow,
My children and I.
See how I run to their aid, Mother,
And lift them with strong arms, on strong legs,
Keep them from harm like a mother tiger
And love them, hold them, bend down to them,
Laugh with them and tease them,
Touch warm skin, ruffle soft hair
As you would have done.
I think of her on that last morning
Alone in a quiet house with my father,
The little dog panting gently by the bed,
Her life slowly lifting away in sunbeams.
Did she hope she would still be there
When we returned from school,
Little brother and I? Did she?
Or did she plead with Death to hurry,
To lift her away from the pain,
The worn-out body that bound her,
Kept her from us while she slept
Her last year away? What would I have done?

Liz Davies

Old Mother

She carries her young deep in her womb
Her heart lies heavy, cold like a tomb
Her eyes have seen misery and pain
She's done her best, so she isn't to blame
Her children she watched over the years
Her life was full of hopes and fears
In her wisdom her judgements were fair
She gave her life and all her care
Her children grew then one day were gone
She was alone without daughter or son
She looked bewildered, her face was worn
Her heart was bleeding, her mind was torn
She stood in the house, at the walls she would stare
Her voice was silent, words couldn't speak
Her head was bowed, her soul was meek
She found herself where it all began
The tears in her eyes suddenly ran
All her life all she had known
Now it was obsolete and outgrown
Left with a lifetime of memories true
Now her life she had to start anew
For she was wise in many ways
And she lived on for endless days
For she is not like any other
She is woman, she is Mother.

Jackie Oung

Tribute To Mothers

We salute her who is called *Mother*
She is filled with love, compassion and so much care
And all that makes a house a happy home
Though often she is taken for granted
Forward she strides with loving smile
Then woman is a mother all her life
When she is small she is mother to the dolls she plays with
Little grown, she is mother to young siblings who dare
More often she plays mother to the man she marries
When children come she is completely into her role
She mothers old parents when weak and pale
The needy, the orphans could have a mother, Teresa she was called
Our Lord was born of a woman, a mother so perfect
Woman is a mother from the beginning to the end.

Prabha Margaret Peters

My Mum And I

Every day is Eid day for Mum and I
Because every day we share a smile
And it lingers for a while
Beneath the beatific sky
A sudden surge of happiness
Is inevitably what I get
And our togetherness begets
A kind of Heaven, no less
And on Mother's Day it's just right
That I should give her flowers
Anticipating happy hours
In the sun's splendid light
She looks so beautiful in her gown
And my heart is filled with peace
She laughs and is at ease
So that I hope she's never down.

Muhammad Khurram Salim

Poem For Lydia

Far from the maddening crowd
Our Lydia be
Honey and silk so softly sits
With book in hand she ponders deep
To bring her nearer to thee

So little time we have to spare
Amongst the continuous onward fare
But sweet in nature she bears
With smiles to share and loving care
Our Lydia be

Slow in motion, light as air
She moves so delicately as ladies dare
To bring to this world all her wares
What would life be without you dear?
Be forever near - our Lydia be.

Thelma Glanville

A Mother's Hands

Tucking a small boy into a warm bed
Soothing a hot brow while stroking his head
Spooning cough syrup and cod liver oil
Stirring pea soup simmering, slow to boil
Kneading and prodding dough when making fresh bread
Spreading jam for kids waiting to be fed.

Grabbing a squirming child ready for flight
Grasping him tight as he kicks and fights
Scrubbing a grubby neck with all her might
Whisking pancake batter, fluffy and light
Dribbling while hot with thick rich honey
Counting out pennies for pocket money.

Craving mouth-watering slices of meat
Baking stuffed apples for a special treat
Rubbing scones with raisins and milk turned sour
Rolling pastry on a bed of flour
Scooping water from sink piled with dishes
Blowing bubbles for kids to make wishes
Hanging wet washing to dry on the line
Tapping rhythms of a nursery rhyme
Dancing fingers teaching long division
Dressing scuffed knees with surgical precision
Easing brush through daughter's unruly locks
Teasing out wool to knit scarves and socks.

Hands once so caring with a capital 'C'
Perpetually busy for you and me
Halted abruptly while still in their prime
Legacy encrusted in sands of time
Hands that spoke volumes as words never do
As they conveyed their message, 'I love you'.

Kathleen Potter

Mother's Day

In years gone by when maids were in service
They were given the third Sunday of Lent
As a holiday to go home to visit Mother
Whom they hadn't seen for the year just spent.

I left the richness of the landed gentry
Walked sorefoot back to my village home
With clogs for feet and no waterproof gown
I trudged with increasing joy to see you, Mom.

You fell upon me with open arms,
'How you've grown, my love. Do they work you hard?'
'Oh Mom, my dearest, how I long for this day
The manse is cold, Madam shows us no regard.'

'We maids sleep beneath one blanket
We rise at 4am to light the fire, clean the grate
Fetch the coal - no breakfast till this job is done
A meagre porridge, then dish washing is our fate.'

'But, my mom dear, it's good to see you
I miss your caring and warm chat
You were so wise to try and stop me
Going over the hill to that habitat.'

'I miss you so, but we must not be sad
Here's a posy of snowdrops pure
I picked as I came along the road
Life is hard, but of you I'm sure.'

Jane McCarty

I Thought That We'd Be Close Again

I never thought that you would die
I thought that we'd be close again
I didn't want to say goodbye
I never thought that you would die
I didn't mean to stay away
My heart is heavy with the pain
I never thought that you would die
I thought that we'd be close again.

Philippa Bower

Mother's Day

A mother's day is never done,
Is what they always say.
She finds a way to complete all tasks
Somehow by the end of the day

She shows love and patience
To her husband and her children.
She manages to always clean and cook,
Every day and not just now and then.

A mother's smile is warm and comforting
As she greets you, her love is always shown
Or when you are hurt or injured,
She lets you know you're not alone.

A mother's love is unconditional,
No matter what you've put her through.
She's always that understanding mother,
That shows she'll always love you.

William Lacewell Jr

Mother's Day (An Appreciation)

A mother's love's a blessing, the songwriter pens
Reality is in essence the lifetime of strains
Noticing the countless times this love is to be measured
Contentedly so when it is richly treasured.

From tiny tot to full-grown adult
Proud to see the accomplishment in orbit
To fetch and carry, never tiring to please
Maternal nature fulfilled, never ill at ease.

To see them grown and with offspring in tow
A realisation with pleasure grow
Handing over the heritage family tradition to offset
Relaxing in the goodness from Heaven beget.

Mother's Day is therefore a time to reflect
Upon unselfish moments so lovingly perfect
Assigned to all of the clan
Mindful no favourite was chosen to plan.

Anthony McGeehan

Thanks

Thanks, Mum, for my life as a child
It wasn't that bad, really quite mild
I was taught my manners
To say 'please' and 'thanks'
It wasn't that bad
Growing up through the ranks
You might even say life was 'cool'
But yes, I hated to go by the rule
I was taught right from wrong
And the do's and the don'ts
You never dared to say 'I won't'
Thanks for teaching me all I know
Now I know where my life is to go
For now I have the key to success
I really will do my very best
Now I can't wait
To become a good mother
So I can pass down the knowledge
From one to another.

Karen Edis

Mum's Letter

I found it in some papers
Stored so long ago
A letter from my mother
And it was good to know
I had this simple message
Written in her hand
Her love preserved forever
A time gap now was spanned

Simple words that mothers say
Still alive from another day
The mum I'd had
Now gone away
Her lovely words
Were here to stay
And with her letter
The love I knew
Before her life
And spirit flew.

Ray Ryan

Mother

Do you remember the day you held me tight
And how I gave you a sleepless night?
Now I'm grown and have a daughter of my own
I know she loves me as much as I love you
And without us both she wouldn't know what to do
This photo reminds me how life used to be
And if it wasn't for you there wouldn't be a me
Take this momento of times gone by
And I know you'll have a little cry
To me you're like a tree, you've lots of arms to cuddle me
I know I've been a pain, yet you love me still the same
You gave me life and God gave me a soul
And between you both you made me whole
You listen to all my troubles and tell me
Not to get into muddles
No matter what I do or say
I know you'll be there every day
So not for today but each and every day
Will always be my mother's day.

This has to be one of the best, unlike all the rest
Cos it's a photo of you and me
And how you would really like us all to be
Your little baby, sorry we can't do that for you
But at least you have your grandchildren and great-grandchildren too
And they truly love you.

Dorothy Healey

I Wrote This For My Mother

Sit with me with twilight half-shut eyes
And think awhile
And let the corners of your mouth curve to gentle smile.
Imagine sitting on a moonlit beach
Looking out at everlasting mill pool sea,
Watching soft tides lap at endless smooth sands at mountain's feet;
Tiny white horses gather on the gentle hush-hush of ocean beat.

Imagine a sunset that paints the sky love-red
And sets the soul on fire.
Feel the warmth of a summer's night and no jacket.
Follow the path to the sand dunes and cross them -
This is where you will find me.
I usually sit on the rocks and skim stones across the little river
That runs out to the sea.

Rebecca Dobson

A Mother's Heart

A mother's heart stores many things
Stored until, a silent tear it brings
A withered flower held in a tiny hand
The spade that built the castle in the sand
A love letter, laughter and the tears.

It stores riches without measure, beautiful and grand
All locked away forever until the Promised Land
Her heart of love which stands the test
Forgetting the grudges, only remembering the best
The sunshine, the refreshing rain and snow
Are gathered treasures more than Man can know.

The first words and steps that Sonny did
Are memories locked with the broken toys he hid
The teaching she gave, showing right from the wrong
And the pleasure it gave when he burst into song
The memories of neighbours who came through the door
All offering their help, when she was so poor.

These memories are her riches beyond earthly measure
So doesn't look far for her buried treasure
Through all the years when problems pressed
In her heart they found comfort and rest
We remember our mother with her memories of us
And the sacrifice she made without any fuss.

Sidney Talbot

Mother's Anxiety

Away from the ocean beach
Mother and her son lived -
A dreary life of distress
Would them thwart all times,
She would be busy in spinning
And weaving from morn till night,
And her son would be out
Into the ocean, grave and vast
As a sailor smart and upright!
The blessed morning sun
She would welcome to fill
Her house with golden beauty infinite.

Often would she steal to the window
And trace the footprints bold
Of her dear son upon the sand;
Soon she got afraid lest
Her son be killed by pirates
Furious and terrible!
From sorrow-clouded eyes
Tears she dropped anon
Unnoticed and her heavy heart
Would be heaving like the rise
And fall of waves dashing
Against the shore in silence profound!
Sea fowls one dusky evening
Up in the air would be rounding and rounding
With bitter notes rough,
Deepening her silent suffering;
Days gone by, yet no hope brightening
At last the golden sun slowly rising
One day creates the splendid moments of beauty
Marking the horizon so mysteriously glowing!
From an anchoring ship at a distance,
Amid many shouts and clamours
Her son's voice faint could she recognise
Quite strangely enough.

Professor Kalyan Ray

My Mum

My mother meant so much to me
As her love for us was plain to see
She always helped and always cared
But mostly she was just always there
She had modern thoughts and was full of fun
Full of stories with all the things she'd done
One of the silliest things that means most to me
Was seeing her decorating the Christmas tree
I can still see her very loving face
. . . Though she always kept us in our place
If we were ever feeling down and sad
She was always easier to talk to than Dad
Then she took unwell and went downhill
Her features showed that she was very ill
We were young and didn't think it was that bad
She'll get better and then we'll all be glad
But then when she was only 38
God took her up to Heaven's gate
Looking back it felt so very wrong
That half of our world had just gone
She will never see all the things I did
Never met my wife or ever seen my kids
I know that as the years go by, oh so fast
My treasured memories of her will always last
And my thoughts for her will always stay
And my love for her grows more every day.

Chris Leith

Staring Bright: The Ages Of Woman

'Last scene of all
That ends this strange eventful history
Is second childishness and mere oblivion
Sans teeth, sans eyes, sans taste, sans everything'
('The Seven Ages of Man' by William Shakespeare)

Greta Garbo glamour at twenty-one
bought with your hard-earned cash. The photographer
placed one hand at your throat above
the white fur wrap with lighting to gloss
your porcelain skin and cold waved jet-black hair.
(Sepia cannot conceal your lipstick's cherry-red).

Your Cary Grant sifted sheet music
at the Saturday market; a country-born lad
on a farm at fourteen in the year you both left school.
Your sister said, '*You could do better.*'
But you started collecting for your bottom drawer;
there was a white wedding on the eve of war.

Your Garbo likeness and your wedding shot
sideboard sentinels to my childhood.
The perfect Fifties' housewife, you
traced templates of a woman's role
onto refractory matter. I am not
the daughter you would have liked me to be.

I keep forgetting to replace the glass;
cracked when you fell over the coffee table
my father never mended. You airbrushed
the time he spent away with another woman
But your forehead rutted like an arid field
and a trough of white ran through your hair.

Sole survivor of your generation
you answer the call of dead voices
as you drift in and out of your dreams.
You wake in a place where you're still twenty-one
and through the kindness of cataract gauzes
you put your red lipstick on.

Carole Alexander

Darling Mum

With your fair complexion
And your brownish auburn hair
Your blue eyes were wonderful
But it was the beauty inside
What was radiant in you
You were a true lady
With all nobleness and gracefulness
But above all you were my mother
So gentle, so kind with me
Always there for any of my problems
You always found the right words
One day, you closed your weary eyes
For so many years now
But you are still in my heart
And it is only now at my age
That I understand you better
You are my darling mum
And nobody deserves more
This sweet and wonderful name
Which is rightly yours.

Victorine Lejeune Stubbs

I Used To Watch You

I used to watch you baking
'Twas a treat to taste when done
I used to watch you cleaning
And thought you were having fun
I saw you make my bed
Each morn after I arose
If you had been my wife
I would gladly have given you a rose.

I used to watch you kiss Daddy
I thought it oh so rude
Yet Mummy I know - in heart
I should not be there to intrude
You made my lunch for school
And prepared my tea each night
Oh Mummy, I didn't deserve you
My chest feels oh so tight.

I used to watch you always
But grown up - those days are past
Oh Mother, how I miss you
Now you reside in Heaven at last
I now weep at your graveside
As I long for those days gone by
When I used to watch you smiling
As even the sun winked its eye.

Oh Mother, I hate your parting
But your memories carry me on
I shall still always watch you
Until I also - am finally gone.

Steve Kettlewell

Poem For Mum

Sole survivor of our Civil War
Awake at last in San Diego
Scene of the past peace, where Father
Retired finally from the field and gave
In his spurs to lie
Parallel at last.

Leaving you in limbo
Dancing in a last
Fling before you
Retire finally from the field and
In California's blossom-hung air
Discover
What you, Mother, had all along.

Jon Elkon

Our Mother's Love

Father lay the golden egg
But Mother - dear Mother, would always cook the goose
We always did what Father said
But Mother - dear Mother, ruled the roost.
And when Father was angry and would scream and yell abuse
Mother's love smothered us, a fact not far from truth.

Father could be nice or mean in many ways
And Father's word was never wrong
Except when Mother had words to say
Then Father - poor Father, would sadly sulk all day
'Father's word is law,' Mother would remind and always say
And we as kids knew the score
That's why we'd gladly all obey.

Yes, a mother's love is often felt
Amidst those who tend to stray
As where Father often answered with the belt
It was left to Mother to smooth the way.

Mother suffered, decades of high an' lows
Especially when Father died of cancer
Upon that cold, bleak, winter's day
And when things got tight and tough
And for a mo' she'd lost her way
She'd smile once more and say,
'You're only poor until you die
But happiness is at my door to stay.'

So a mother's love to us
Was an eternal heart of endurance and affection
Applying, occasionally, her tools of trade
The guiding hand of sweet correction
And that is why to us, our mother's love, will ne'er fade.

Glenwyn Peter Evans

My Mother - A Tribute

With the sleekness of a black panther
A beautiful woman poured into red chiffon
Midnight hair and sapphire eyes
How I admired you, needed you.

For when I became burdened and laden
You tried to carry that weight on your own shoulders
As you knew it was too heavy to carry alone.

And when deep sadness engulfed me
You were wise and reminded me
That no one said pain doesn't hurt
But it heals - because it simply has to.

Then when my heart shrivelled into a hardened little walnut
You gave me the strength to set it free
To follow a dream.

So when I think of courage
I think deeply of you
My mother, my mum, a lady.

Beverley Harknett

My Time Over Again

Mother, where are my drainpipes you washed the other day?
I had a ten bob note in the pocket I saved from my pay
The Brylcreem's nearly empty, can't get a proper DA
Mother, you don't listen to a bleeding word I say
I won't be home too early, don't let me sleep too late
That's how I lost my last job, Mother you're a hard one to educate.

Now she is gone, those words I regret a thousand times and more
Perhaps these words will reach her, she will know I love her for sure
I put flowers on her grave most Sundays, once a week
If only I could have my time over, I would know just how to speak
God bless you Mother, this is a worse world without you that is for sure
I still can't find my things, but that don't seem to matter anymore.

John Bennetts

In Her Eyes

When I look in the mirror, what do I see?
This older lady looking back at me
How the years have flown past at such a fast pace
When her reflection revealed a much younger face
And I can see in her eyes as she gives me a frown
That life has had its ups and it's sure had its downs
But I can see in her eyes and it's positively clear
That she has been held very dear

I can see behind her eyes where her memories lie
There's a library of tales as she utters a sigh
It's in her eyes

When I look in the mirror, what do I see?
This older lady looking back at me
Yet someone has loved her throughout all these years
And I can see in her life there have been few lonely tears
Just behind her eyes where her memories lie
There's a library of tales as she utters a sigh
Yet the smile she now gives as she looks back at me
Says that was then, this is now and what will be, will be
That it's with pride that someone can even reach this stage
Cos it's all in the mind, this thing they call age
It's in her eyes.

Rita Bridgman

Who Would Be A Mother?

Who would be a mother in this day and age?
Never-ending tasks, oceans of tea
A perpetual source of constant rage
Little children running free!

Bedtime bliss leaves time to clear
The massacre of toys
Of earlier games and tantrums near
Planning tomorrow's ploys.

A mother's a confessor and maker of peace
A diplomat, sometimes a monster for teens
Spoiling and restricting, supposed free lease
A lender of money without end or means.

It's hard being a mother, never winning
But oh what a loss would I have had
Should an experience have no beginning?
Still, I think, a mother feels always glad.

Who would be a mother in this day and age?
Personally not missing it for the world
Remembering my mother's words on a previous page
Looking at pages of albums unfurled.

When my daughters become mothers
Perhaps my words are echoed no end
Advice always true, there can be no others
Sure of my stance, yet easy to bend.

Pauline Pickin

New Start
(In memory of my mum, Dilys, who died from kidney cancer)

I was so hurt, so torn apart by grief
Fighting back tears I could not weep
As I watched my mother die in pain
Of the nightmare of cancer wasting her away.

I held her hand and stroked her face
Looked into her eyes through a tearful haze
Spent minutes and hours and days and days
As I watched her slowly slip away.

When she died, at first I felt relief
I was numb with shock and disbelief
Which slowly turned to pain and grief
So lost, now my mum had her final sleep.

An empty feeling, I couldn't eat or sleep
A physical pain that hurt so deep
Like a part of me had been cut away
Haunted by her agony every day.

I never thought that I could get through
I felt panic and didn't know what to do
I longed to escape from my misery
And have things back how they used to be.

I had to put her out of my mind
Which felt like a betrayal of some kind
I had to get through each day, somehow
Without falling apart or breaking down.

My chest felt heavy with unshed tears
Full of anxiety and groundless fears
With trembling hands and an aching heart
I knew I had to make a brand new start.

I had to put my mum in the past
Though my love for her will always last
She will always be with me in my mind
She was so loving, tender and kind.

I have to forget the pain she went through
And remember all that she could do
With a simple look she could melt my heart
And I know she would be proud of my new start.

Carol Ponting

Cuddles

When a child says, 'Mum, can I have a cuddle?'
And looks into your eyes with that gleam of love
Then with a melting heart you hold in your arms
One little bundle of softness that kisses your cheek
A little arm round your neck does softly enfold
Then with a soft sigh eyes do close, a dream to weave
Curly head and pink cheeks with all those charms
Asleep in a cuddle, lies a child so meek
Cradled in a mother's arms.

John Clarke

Stuck In The Middle

Imagine what it would be like
To be stuck at the age of sixteen
Not yet an adult
But no longer a child.
But that's what I've got to do
Being a caring mother
Wondering whether he'd rather be
Like Jack and the Beanstalk or
Like Peter Pan in Neverland
He's trying ever so hard
To fulfil all the hopes of achievements
Being expected of him
But yet he has to make major decisions
Like whether or not
To join the race to lose virginity
To take up a human vice
To aim for an ASBO award
And what about responsibilities?
Old enough for some
Too young for others
Who decides?
Perhaps he should
He's ever so fearless
Unlike good, old, cautious me
Imagine how he must feel
What with all the peer pressure
And that from me
It must be ever so confusing
Being stuck in the middle.

Eunice Ogunkoya

Eighty Years
(For Mum 28/3/05)

Now, six years turning
Part of creation's
Change aware, of you
Dear 'special friend'
Now, in silence when
You come from light
Higher vibration where
You live the holy life
Easter, a time of
Remembering movement
On from pain, 'death', new
Life where you stand again
Young, running, dancing
Joy has come in the morning
Still 'special friends'
Knowing special life where
Love shall never die.

George Coombs

Mother's Day

Many may feel surrounded with grief
Many may watch for the postman to open the gate
Inspiration only make-belief
Someone may call with violets blue
Someone spare a thought for the lonely who
Would like a posy of flowers to say
'Thinking of you on Mother's Day'
Knowing someone, perhaps all alone
Bunch of daffodils
Wouldn't go wrong
Little bunch in child's tiny hand
Cheery word
Smile of a child
Won't cost much
'Twill last for many a day
The cheer of a child
Bringing sunshine to a mother
Lonely, forgotten on Mother's Day
Show kindness to the aged and lonely
Take time to read and pray
The seed you sow will grow you know
We too may be old and lonely some day.

Frances Gibson

Lovely In Red

How lovely you looked today
Dear Mother
All in red and your hair a silver-grey
Sound asleep now
With a smile on your face
Lay to rest now dear Mother
This is our last goodbye
Until my time comes
And I lay by your side
Take care of my little angel
Who sits up there beside you
Take her hand and she will guide you
You're gone now but will never
Be forgotten,
You'll always be here in our hearts.

Amanda Houghton

Mother

Here's to you dear Mother
For the help you've given me
I want to say 'thank you'
And how much you mean to me.

You've put up with so much
I'm sorry that had to be
I've become a new person now
So you'll be proud of me.

I used to mess around
Sometimes be a clown
But that was me
Just kidding around.

Now I'm a bit older
And responsible to be
The kind and generous person
I once used to be.

Love from Michelle.

Michelle Crozier

Mums Eh?

My kitchen is a smelly place
It's so unfit for the human race
The bin bags lay across the floor
There's jam and cheese upon the door.

The bread's so mouldy, it's kind of green
And even the kettle's steam's unclean
The tiles are black, the fridge door too
There's creatures living here
That should be in a zoo
And the air smells like they do
It's really quite a bit like poo!

I'm sitting here upon my chair
Looking at the mess out there
I'm sad and flat, so full of despair
I really wish I could repair
The damage done to my right toe
So I could get up
And move and go
Into the kitchen, that's so dirty
And clean it, but my toe's so hurty.

I think I'll do what must be done
Pick up my phone and call my mum
I know she'll moan and make a fuss
But if I am nice I'm sure she'll rush
And come over with some gloves and bleach
And sprays that smell so lush in peach
And freshen up my kitchen so
So I won't have to move and go
And hurt some more my throbbing toe.

I'll just sit here and call my mum
Yes, that is what must be done
She really is my bestest chum
And I'm her special number one.

I hope I'm being not too mean
But she really loves to clean, then find the dirt that can't be seen
I have a plan, maybe it's mad
But when she comes, I'll appear sad
And tell her the whole house smells bad.

She'll grab her cloth and her washing stuff
And scrub the house, she'll rub and buff
And when the house is clean enough
She'll stop to moan and huff 'n' puff
But I won't care, I'll blame my toe
And tell her that I couldn't go
And do the things that she does best
That thing that fills my house with zest
Anyway, I need to rest, my throbbing toe
Yes, that's the best.

And when my house again is clean
I won't be tight and I won't be mean
I'll call her up with thanks and praise
And thank her for her clean-up days
And tell her she's a wicked mum
And that her son's a lazy bum!
She won't agree
She'll just say I'm not
Because I'm the only son she's got
She'll say she really loves me so
And we'll both blame my throbbing toe
Cos mums eh, they simply know!

Andy Wheeler

Mums

Mums are there when you are sad
Mums are there when you are bad
Mums are there when you need advice
Mums are there when you have headlice.

Mums make us happy, mums change our nappies
Mums clean our rooms, mums make us bloom
Mums are like angels, they guide us through all
Mums are like angels, they catch us when we fall.

Some people's mums live far away
Some people don't have time to say,
That there's a deep love that burns inside
A love for our mums that we cannot hide.

Sophie Greig

Mum

My mum, I give you thanks from my heart
For giving my life such a wonderful start
You do not realise the happiness you bring
You are the one whose praise I sing
Giving so much love and support
Special things that can never be bought
Always there to listen and guide
Often your true feelings you had to hide
Teenage years were troublesome at times
You only wanted to guide me through life's landmines
Respecting each other so no bridges to mend
My wonderful mother and invaluable friend
That is why you really are unique
So strong for me when I have felt weak
These words hopefully explain what I don't always say
I want to make your life special in every way
Each day you deserve all the very best
To me Mum, you really are the greatest.

Anne Sackey

For My Mother

Nearly two years ago, not long after Christmas,
You died and a dark corner of my heart closed forever.
I think of you in those occasional times you appeared happier
Than a skylark's flight, temporarily escaping the war's nightmares.

Somehow it seems it was always some time in midsummer,
The sun shimmering across the brilliant estuary water at Maldon,
The boats bobbing and bubbling in the horizon's hot cauldron
And all your children playing and laughing in the castle park
                                                      at Colchester.

Seasons swam through you like fish
Swarming in spawning shoals in the black sea of your head
Cruelly conscious of lost loves now long-dead.
I saw in your eyes dreams rot like waste food on a serving dish.

You are gone now, but not forgotten, your constant kindness
Still present in the continually flowering gardens of our remembrances.

Roland Gurney

My Lost Mum
(For my mum who has dementia)

Where have you gone
The person I knew?
Your presence is there
But it isn't you.

There are moments it seems
When you return once more
But it's fleeting now
And it's not like before.

I miss you so much Mum
And yet you are there
You look at me sometimes
And I am aware
Of the sadness inside you
As you hold that stare.

If I could bring you back now
Like it used to be
I would cherish the time
Spent with me.

And if I could free you from confusion
That took you away
Give you back your rightful claim
To pride and dignity.

I would do it, Mum
I would do it for you
To save all the sorrow
That you are now going through.

Patricia Dawson

A Mother's Love

There is a gift which gives perpetual bliss
The human life has nothing to compare
A mother's love, a gift from Heaven is this
To lavish on her offspring everywhere.

How sweet, the bonding of two kindred souls
A secret shared, what depth of mystery
Yet, now a lifetime of devotion rules
With early days of playfulness and glee.

And, as one grows, to labour on Life's way
A constant stream of blessings still arrives
That, even if some evil we essay
A mother's love replenishes our lives.

What debt we owe and how may we
Repay the one who fed us in the womb?
By caring for all weak humanity
And to despairing needy, giving room.

For we have life in every vital nerve
From one who gave herself in selfless love
With meek humility and no reserve
Echoing the divine life from above.

Vere Collins

My Hardworking Mother

My mother works all day
Not a moan in sight
Does her due
Washing, ironing
Black-lead the range
Empties the ashes
Shopping
Works on the bills
To be paid
Washes in the old tub
That's my mother
Who deserves a medal.

Alan Hattersley

My Mum
(Dedicated to my mum, Lorna Kathleen Stallard, aged 98)

Was through a child's eyes I could see
How beautiful Mum was to me
Her tall, slim frame and dark brown hair
Would make the world turn round and stare
She had that twinkle in her eyes
That shamed the stars up in the skies.

I used to sit and wonder then
Would it happen once again?
Could I create the same allure
If I could only look like her
She'd charm the birds up in the trees
I spent my childhood at her knees
Listening to the songs she sang
And tales she'd tell of when she was young.

In wintertime so cold outside
We couldn't wait to get inside
And when I close my eyes I see
The room that means so much to me
Where by the fire we'd gather round
Waiting for the nights to come
And fondly waiting for the sound
Of the voice and the love that is my mum!

Joy Toms

A Mother's Wish . . .

Debbie and Robbie are lovers, if I may speak so bold
They stay in a lot, because outside it's so cold
A tall handsome boyfriend was Debbie's true wish
Her knees really trembled from his first loving kiss.

The air went 'electric' each time that they met
Her arms sliding around him, when they started to pet
The sun had to blush, the stars closed their eyes
To their passionate moanings and wonderful sighs.

It's springtime again and all the world loves a lover
'Don't get ideas, he's a friend,' she told her dear mother
It's lovely to see Debs, dressed up for her date
Now Robbie's her boyfriend and a very good mate.

How much she liked him, Debbie will never disclose
But her happiness unfolds - like a newly born rose
Debbie's really dumbstruck, no more can be said
Her 'flyboy' dear lover, has asked her to wed!

Our Eileen, her mother, says, 'We must do things right -
So save up your money, for a wedding, that's white!'
Her dad, poor old Malcolm, moans, 'It's a bit of a poser
A wedding that's 'white' will cost four thousand or over.'

Her mother shouts loud, 'Blood's thicker than water
We'll sell the whole house, for our darling daughter.'
'Don't think of the cost, but what you'll save.'
Her dad thought about that, smiled, then decidedly 'gave'.

They've saved up some money, used more than they'd 'hid'
'Make all your arrangements, we'll do you proud kid.'
They're having an RAF wedding, with planes flying past
Mother smiled, hugs daughter. She's getting married - *at last!*

Robert Hessey

Mum

Mum is wonderful
Mum is kind
Mum is gentle
She is all mine
She makes me laugh
She makes me cry
With a heart
A heart of gold
With her mind
Her mind of soul
But most of all
She's all mine.

Angela Cole

Mothers
(For mothers everywhere, including my mum)

On this Mother's Day
Let me stay awhile
And bathe in that real smile
To mothers everywhere give thanks
The gold in their hearts
You can't find in banks
And may you in me
See somebody
In adulthood as well as baby boy
I remember when you gave me my first toy
Through all my scenes of childhood
I remember you as someone good
You gave me life
You gave me food
And that is why I'd like to say, on this special day
That I hope you're proud to call me son.
As I am proud to call you Mum.

Alan Pow

Mum

Mum, Mum, Mum, many times a day
Do you ever wish you could
Change your name instead of 'Mum'?
You do your chores as they play
Today until now, has been quiet and good
Then silence broken - where is Mum?
Peace shattered, noise around
Where is Mum to be found?
Snatching a few minutes alone
Not for long this precious time
As on your knees young ones do climb
They want a drink or are feeling bored
I wish they would play indoors
But all I hear is, 'Mum, Mum, Mum,' all day
I must stay calm and have my say
But they do love me every day.

Sheila Waller

An Angel

Afraid of the dark, all alone in my bed
Shadows playing tricks inside my head
The sheets feel cold, it's damp once again
I've made a mistake, I hope it won't stain.

I tell myself that I am not to blame
I am worried, upset and full of shame
What if my father finds out tonight?
At the very thought my heart beats with fright.

Nowhere to turn, each side now numb
Then in creeps an angel - my loving mum
She always understood, no need to explain
With her tender love she removed my shame.

I climbed out of bed, holding her arms
I felt safe and protected, inside feeling calm,
'It's all right now, love, don't worry,' she said.
'You'll soon be back in a warm, clean bed.'

My heart slowed down, I was afraid no more
My mother had done this many times before
Tucking me in half asleep, more or less
She gently kissed me and whispered, 'God bless!'

Gerard Jones

Frances Mary

The Lord walked in His garden
To attend a lily fair
The fragrance was so beautiful
The growth of beauty rare.

The lily was pure and holy
A mother, good and true
Her name was Frances Mary
Loved by many, not a few.

Her loveliness strengthened others
Purer lives to lead
Her sweetness blessed a little home
Where she was loved indeed.

Surely I'll always remember
Her love and care for me
So precious was her presence
And her smile for all to see.

But the Lord had need to take her
To adorn His portals fair
In one of the many mansions
He has risen to prepare.

And by and by He's coming
From the heavenlies above
For the ransomed in His garden
Precious souls bought with His blood.

It will be a lovely bouquet
When we all are gathered there
Bound by love eternal
In Jerusalem so fair.

Doreen Reeves

Mother

You are gentle, sweet and kind
Another like you would be hard to find
To us children you are strong
Teaching us right from wrong
Showing each of us things to do
Imparting to us your point of view
Giving a love that's really meant
Hoping we grow up strong and decent
And live our lives right to the end
Loving each other as relation and friend
Words of wisdom on how to live
Words that only a mother can give
Give to us children when we part
Give to us children from your heart.

Diana Daley

Mums

Mums
Are made
Of everything good
They are our diamonds
They are our gold
They are the rainbows
And the flowers on the stall
Mums make our lives easier
By being there for us
My mum is no longer with me
But I know she is my angel
That watches over me.

Carolie Cole Pemberton

Dear Mum

Although no longer of this Earth
We remember you with love
This past year has flown so fast
As you took one breath, the last
When that time came to slip away
We fondly remember you still
To offer up a prayer this day
To say the things we meant to say
Be at peace and free from pain
Until that day we meet again - God bless.

Gary Murphy

A Mother's Love

A grandchild's kiss is sweet and loving
A bear hug from a son . . . comforting
A friend's peck . . . a greeting on meeting
An illicit kiss . . . tantalising
Hubby's love, rewarding and sharing
A mother's love . . . constant and caring.

Valerie Ovais

My Mum Was Always There

My mum was always there
She knew my secret self
Long distance or next door
It made no odds to her.

'What's the matter darling?'
Came over on the phone
Whatever troubled me
From far away or near.

Now I'm sixty-seven
No longer have a mum
Last night she slipped away
To be reborn again.

The tears are in my eyes
I miss her just so much
But Mum, I don't deny
Your right to go away.

I have my memories
I'll always hold them dear
And hopefully we'll meet
Along the future track.

Thank you for my childhood
And for the growing years
Where I had your support
Your love, no matter what.

Corin Jasmine Dienes

My Mother Taught Me The Meaning Of Words

My mother taught me the meaning of words
How they have power and pull and take flight like birds
How a man can write down a phrase
A structural sentence or winding word maze
And long after he is gone be remembered and praised.
A single letter or line, any is fine
Pen to paper and typewriter ribbon
Show exactly what care and thought has been given.

David Constable

Kissing Roses

We were walking in the park
On a Sunday afternoon
When she suddenly stopped and kissed a rose
Splendidly in bloom.

She just leaned over and kissed it
Heedless of passers-by
Tall and proud on a slender stem
Fragile and soon to die.

Never tell me she's lying
All alone in the dark
I know that she's kissing roses
Roses in the park!

Tina Molli

This Illustration : A Study In Desolation

He took his mother's ashes to bed that night
Still contained in its crematoria coffer (of purple and white)
Slept in her bed till the early morn
Hugged it to his chest through his depressing and dismal plight
It had been a strange day with nothing but noise getting in the way
He felt he had little to live for anyway
- When his only compatriot - the one he adored, had departed
Leaving him insecure with time on his hands; a lifespan to be endured
He awoke in the early hours - still clutching the urn
Wondering which way his life would now turn
For there was nothing left; not anymore
Not without her presence waiting for him at the kitchen door
She was the only one in the whole wide world, who shared his name
Brought comfort: Aloof/isolated, they were the same
Nothing more remained to placate him
For the desolation that now overcame

Alan Knott

Pretty Girl

Oh so loved and precious daughter by Mum and Dad
Who kept you safe and secure in their love
No longer do you stay in that environment
In the dark of night, someone took you away from your beloved family.

Our tears do flow and mingle with the family that love you so
We all hold on tightly in the fight to get you back, pretty girl,
For we know that everything of beauty is shunned
To make way for greed and evil deeds
But do not be afraid, pretty girl, for our prayers will be answered

And soon you will be home once more
In your loving circle of family and friends
Safe and secure, but you will have had experiences
For one so young in how the world really is.

Julia Holden

Steve

A special person, a special place
A smile on one's face
You are still with us all in your own special way

We are all gathered here to be with you today
When we think of you
We think of the one
And remember a special friend, brother, uncle and son

You are here and you are now
You rest peacefully as if sleeping
Thoughts of you always
And for every day ours for keeping.

Marina Reeves

Dannielle

Look at you, looking up at me
A vision of beauty and you're only three
Crystal eyes, blue as the Med sea
Hair blonde and curly, tied up with a bow
A little round face smiles all aglow
Full of adventure, enjoying life to the full
Lots to endure as you go on your way
New lessons to learn with every new day
Manners, kindness, learning to share
Of daily life, you are already aware
I gaze in wonder, perfection I see
Pretty as a picture and as bold as can be
Big school in September
You will soon be four
Tears in Mum's eyes, that's for sure
How lucky am I, to be your nan
Proud for all to see
Knowing I love you and without a doubt
Wonderful you - loves me.

Janet Granger

For Jake - Born Prematurely

Sweet babe, your breath a fading sigh
Is borne like gossamer
Upon a gentle breeze . . .
You are but a hair's breadth away
As you slip peacefully
Into your final sleep.
Your life is over ere it has begun
Oh, that I could hold you,
Cuddle you, breathe for you
And will you back to life again!
Your tiny form so perfect
Will never feel my arms around you
Sweet innocence, a very special boy.
My love wings heavenwards
To your bright star in the sky . . .
Sleep my angel, peace my angel
As I whisper, 'Goodbye . . .'

Joanne Burns

Daughter . . . Lisa-Marie

Blessed are we
With the gift
Of you.

Female
Beautiful . . .
Softness
Weaving
Its way to
Many hearts.

Careful;
Cautious with
A hint of bravado.

Person of
Many layers
Analytically
Considering the
Possibilities.

Shared laughter
Of the absurd
Pride spills over
If not kept in check.

Never a burden
But always a joy
Dear one.

Marie McCarthy

She Is There For Me
(Dedicated to Julianne)

I have a loving daughter
Sweet and fair
Though she has loved ones of her own
She often phones
She is there for me.

When she bounces in unannounced
Full of humour and bright chatter
Helping with the chores
Even though ill health she bears alone
She is there for me.

I know she easily tires
But does not complain
Too busy working the day away
Yet always finds time to call in on her way
She is there for me.

Her life is a troubled one
Borne with cheerfulness and courage
Yet laughter emits from her beautiful eyes
Which are as blue as the heavenly skies
She is there for me.

How lucky I am to know her
In my twilight years
For no mother could possibly want for more
Such a daughter, so kind and thoughtful to the core
Bless her, for always being there for me.

Gwyneth Scott

The Last Picture Show
(Dedicated to Bernard Groom who left us 16th October 2002)

A pile of faded photographs
Elastic band removed
Past to present
Fighter pilot of squadron drill
English born and bred flew off to a Canadian home
Comrades and friends in familiar surround
Strangers of distant faces to Trevor and I
Uncle Bernard Groom
Entertainer and photographer, loved by so many
In a land so far away
Devoted to our mum
Brother and sister parted, but very much in love
Both now joined as one
Lying peacefully side by side
Sons of Iris Groom
The descendants of your sister you left behind
Nigel and Trevor receive
A first class delivered brown parcel
Which contains a list of lost secrets
Crumpled and creased
To be slowly put together, piece by piece
Inside this collection of memories
We both can only imagine
These treasured moments of days gone by
To try and remember of just how it was
In this your very last picture show
Found in a selection of black and white glory
Is the brave decorated man of the R.A.F
Whom we are so proud
Thanks so much Uncle for letting us in
A small part of your life.

Nigel Astell

Our Dearest Mother

You are our mother who loves us all
From the big ones, down to the very small
You are everything in which we hoped
And we marvel at the way you coped.

In your long and varied life
You were a devoted mother and wife
And when your husband was away
You managed to carry on day by day.

We all love you very much
With your sweetest words and your gentle touch
Your generosity was so overwhelming
Your voice to us was so very calming.

In later years you suffered with pain
But you struggled through again and again
And when it became too much to bear
You left us on Earth, to be with others so dear.

And now you have relief from the pain
We'll never forget you and we'll see you again
In Heaven with others we know you love
We know you'll be watching from your place above.

You're still our mum, there is no doubt
That's what your life's been all about
And we will recall those happier days
When you were with us in so many ways.

We know you've gone to a happier place
And we thank the Lord for all His grace
That He took you when you were so ill
But you left a space no one can fill.

Edna Adams

Welcome

Welcome baby to our world
And welcome to our hearts
You lay beneath your mother's heart
Now learn to live in ours
We welcome you

Welcome baby to our world
And may it be for you
A world of love, of peace and joy
May every day renew
Your welcome.

Patricia Ammundsen

Forty Years On

It started off with *paper*
The second year was *cotton*
Then came *leather, fruit* and wood
I'm sure you've not forgotten
Six was *sugar* sweet or *iron*
Then came *wool* or *copper*
Bronze and *willow*
Tin and *steel*
You'd still not come a cropper
Silk, or *linen* next then *lace*
Ivory - crystal - china
Oh how the anniversaries race
But there is nothing finer
Then *silver, pearl* and *coral*
And still you're feeling great
Now, forty years of smiles and tears
Today you celebrate
But there are still more years ahead
Through *sapphire* on to *golden*
Then *emerald - diamond - platinum*
By then you'll be quite 'olden'.

As you prepare to wine and dine
We hope you're feeling groovy
This is the time for us to sign
Best wishes on your ruby!

Sheila Allen

Blessed Child

Her name is Faye alias Fifi and Dolly
Sometimes she answers to Fie or Polly

She chatters non-stop in a language unknown
We respond with words that mimic her own

Fleet of foot, if, at times unsteady
She rushes around at the ready

To dart through a door or baby gate
As if to say 'No time to lose, no time to wait'

Rescued, she laughs, she's enjoyed the game
And will do the same again and again

Fearless she climbs both stair and chair
'Look at me,' she grins, 'I'm a big white bear'

Her impish smile and winsome ways
Gladden my heart, enrich my days

Oh little child, oh spirit bright
Thank you for bringing your blessed light.

Shelagh Clare James

To My Dad

As a child you held my hand
And guided me along
You helped me build my character
And taught me right from wrong.

You made me face my problems
As each one showed its face
Directed me to find my goal
At a steady even pace.

The lessons that you gave me
Right from the very start
Discussions, disagreements, love
This knowledge you'd impart.

I hope that in the years to come
My children will be glad
That with all the things that you taught me
I became just like my *dad!*

Farina May Jenkins

Your Dad

Let's not be sad when remembering your dad
He always had a smile
Whatever you wanted, he'd put in the effort
And go that extra mile.

On birthdays, at Christmas and Easter too
He'd ask what you want and get it for you
To put a smile upon your face
Not a moment with you did he ever waste.

He wanted what was best for you
And always tried real hard
To be there in your times of need
You were always in his heart.

He held you tight in arms of love
He wiped away your tears
His words of comfort and soothing touch
Would take away your fears.

He was so proud of you, your dad
You were always on his mind
And even though now he's not here
He'll be watching over you, you'll find.

He's happy now, no pain or hurt
No sadness in his life
For him be strong and do your best
Let him be your guiding light.

Joanne Jervis

My Daughter

I held you close when you were a baby,
Cradled you safely many years ago,
You were such a lovely little lady,
Right from the beginning I loved you so.

So quickly into a toddler you grew,
That infant child seemed to grow up so fast,
Became a teenager before I knew,
Now grown up, so swiftly the time has passed.

Today, you have two children of your own,
Two little boys growing up just like you,
Not babies anymore, for they have grown,
And I love them as much as I love you.

Giving birth to you made me a mother,
It showed me what real love is all about,
Only you that made me a grandmother,
And of you all I am immensely proud.

Gilly Jones

My Son

Wet at both ends, with a cry to break glass
Charming when sleeping, peaceful at last.

My opinion of babies as a young working wife
Then *I* was pregnant, it changed my whole life!

My baby was different, I thought him a king
His behaviour was perfect, his praises I'd sing.

I've still sung his praises as the years hurried by
If he met with a challenge, I knew that he'd try.

He's made money, it's vanished again and again
But he's never lost heart, just smiled through the rain.

The years have been kind to him, I think to me too
He's a son to be proud of - yes, baby, it's you!

Joyce Jones

Family History

She found a box of photographs
So ancient, they were full of laughs
'Just look at great-aunt Rhoda's hat
Who is that man with the long beard?
I'd never wear bathers like that -
I think that they look really weird
I like this one. Who are they, please?
It says 'Four Generations' here.
A toddler sitting on the knees
Of an old lady with white hair
And long black dress. Another two
Are standing there. Is that child you?'

'No, that's Gamma when she was young
And that's her mum, your great-gamma.
This one's *her* mother, great-great-gran
If you can get it round your tongue
This is your great-great-great-gamma.
When was she born? Now, let me see:
I think in eighteen-forty-three.'
Wow!

Gwen Joselin

Gift Of Love

Darling baby, born of love
At last we see your face
Reality of many dreams
You've come to take your place
So delicate, so beautiful
Your features and your eyes
Are you destined to be famous
Successful, rich and wise?
All these things are possible
But I know one thing is true -
Never will we know more joy
Than came that day with you!

Shirley Allen

Special One

I remember the first day I held you
You were lovely as can be
A special gift you came to us
I held you tenderly
When you started smiling
You made us smile too
When you started laughing
We laughed along with you
We held your hand to encourage you
To take your first few steps
The day you walked towards us
We were proud as we could be
Then you started talking
And we had lots of fun
Nursery rhymes and little songs
We taught you one by one
Over the years we watched you
And as we look with pride
We see a happy family standing by your side
So as your birthday comes again
We remember the joy and laughter
Love to our special daughter
Who will always be our number one.

Jean Adam

To Holly

As grey skies of February faded
And snowdrops beautified the garden
All around was pale and shrouded
Soon to blossom, perfumed hues
As birds on high, heralded their springtime news.

This welcome girl-child, born this month
Is the very essence of the newborn spring
Softly folded in her mother's arms, to bring
Untold joys, as she joins the multitude of those yet to be
Create a life of love, will she!

Dorothy Athorn

Sweet Music

Mother Music
Mother Music
You sing such sweet Love songs
Mother Music
'Mother', Music
It is for You I long.

April Dickinson-Owen

Ella And Freddie

Ella is now three
And Freddie is now one
These two loveable children
Are a blessing to behold
Ella has her doll's house
Freddie is into trains
As he gurgles and she shouts
Out her commands to her mother
Becoming very bossy is Ella
The eldest of the two
She pulls around her brother
And orders him to feed
Pushing a bottle into his mouth
He cries with the force
Mother shouts, 'Hold on Ella, he's only young.'
As Ella shouts, 'Sorry Mum.'
But these two are a blessing to behold
Ella goes to playgroup
Also goes to Sunday School
Freddie will start soon at a school
When he's older and wiser
Then he won't put up with the pulling of hair
And being dragged by his legs
A blessing to count every day
As their young lives go on.

Elaine Day

Luke

On a cold November morn
Our little grandson Luke was born
His arrival seven weeks early
Hair all dark, wet and curly.

An incubator start for him
Lights so very, very dim
Keeping him warm and snug
We'll have to wait for that first hug.

Of his safe arrival we were all glad
Especially proud Mum and Dad
Their family now complete
Just sister Jessica for him to meet.

Visitors came with cards and parcels
To see this latest arrival
Outfits tiny, teddies galore
Luke wouldn't want for anything more.

Gillian D'Arcy

Jack

A beaming smile
A wrinkled nose
Chubby knees
Tiny toes
That's Jack.

Looking for
His favourite toy
Tornado on legs
Our little boy
That's Jack.

The biggest eyes
And softest skin
With cuddles
You could melt in
That's Jack.

But most of all
He's ours to hold
A joy, an angel
Good as gold
That's Jack.

Mary Daines

Baby It's You

Baby it's you again, why do you cry so?
I put you down a short while ago
It is the middle of the night
What is the matter, are you catching fright?

Baby it's you again, why do you cry so
While being pushed out in the sunshine so?
You were well-fed before we came out
It is a good job you cannot scream and shout.

Baby it's you again, why do you cry so
When I am trying to give you your tea?
Is there something so very wrong with me?
The doctor says you are really fine
Have you something upon your mind?

Keith Powell

Mother

My mother is always there for me
For tears and laughter that we shared
Over the years there has been a lot
Of problems and times we'd rather forget.

The times when I was a child are good
The holidays on the beach
Where we stood looking out to sea
Like time stood still for her and me.

The favourite place that we both still share
Going there together when times were hard
Coming on holiday with me when I was alone
With two children to bring up on my own.

Always helping me move on
Still there now I have brushed myself down
Got on with my life
She's still there, always mine to share.

She's getting old now and for her I care
Going round and helping her out
Taking her shopping and for a ride in the car
Getting the children to know her.

My mum's always been there for me
I try to impress upon the children what it's like
I try to be like her for their sake
The values I was taught I pass on to them.

I only hope I can do the same
To bring them up as she did me
My mother, I love her
And she loves me.

Janet Jannaway

Our Shirley's Birthday . . .

March the thirtieth is The Red Letter Day
Still another . . . anniversary's on the way . . .
Our far distanced but joyful love to you we relay
To us all you brighten up days that are grey.

There's so many memories . . . hard where to begin
Baby-blue eyes, blonde hair and a cheeky grin
An infectious laugh . . . you are a daily vitamin
Your loveable nature has us all in a spin.

Those early years of so much happiness and play
Then you saved up sixpence . . . to run away . . .
All the cuddles, all the hugs, the love you display
Deeply involves emotions and senses wobble astray . . .

Your deep naturalness that others strive to attain
The freshness and wonky humour . . . is our gain
Though, on occasion, your batteries do drain
You always bounce back, my little chilblain . . .

That there is you, our youngest daughter, our ray of sunshine
The happiness of this special day be thine
Our eternal love, as always, oh daughter o' mine
As . . . as once again you're . . . twenty-nine . . .

J Fred Jackson

I'd Like To Say

My dad is getting older
Each and every day
So I'd like to take a moment
There's some things I'd like to say

I'd never be where I'm at
Without your helping hand
With advice that you give freely
When I hung my head and cried

You told me to never give up
Or to throw away my dreams
But you'd love me no matter what
You'd love me just the same

So in writing this poem
I share with you
The dream I love the most
And to write 'I love you Daddy'
In this simple little poem.

Margaret McGinty

For A Loving Mom

For all my life you have been there
To guide me through and show you care

You're the rock I can lean on
A sturdy shoulder I can cry on

You brought sunshine to all my mornings
And brought light to all my evenings

You've shown God's love in everything you do
And taught us good values by example too.

You bore it all through the good and bad
And helped us get well when we were sick and sad.

The best of a friend you're always near
To laugh and cry, to tease and cheer.

You're always there to give all you have
To attest and manifest God's eternal love.

An angel without wings, that's what you are
That God has picked from among the stars.

No one else will ever be like you
For you are the only one and the greatest too!

A love like yours there will be no other
And I'm proud to claim you are my mother!

Rachelle Arlin Credo

My Little Sister

I have a little sister
Susie is her name,
She's always into mischief,
Always ready for a game.

She's a terror in the garden
Flowers aren't safe when she is near
Even when she scatters flower heads about
And Dad is cross, she knows no fear.

Indoors, it's not safe to leave her for long
Mum's always saying, 'Where's that Sue?'
Yesterday she was ages in the toilet.
What did we find? Flannels down the loo!

But when bedtime's here and bath time's over
Off to dreamland she'll soon be bound.
When stories are read, prayers are said
And hugs and kisses are given
Then she slumbers sweetly without a sound.

Ruth Berry

For The Loss Of A Mother

Yours was the womb that bore me
Yours were the arms that held me
Yours was the heart that loved me
Yours was the love that nourished me
Yours was the love that grew to embrace our ever growing family
And yet was so personally mine
Dear Mum, now that you have left this mortal world
May God's angels take this love and weave it into a blanket
To keep you warm whilst you sleep peacefully in their arms
Sweet dreams Mum
God bless.

Christine Collins

A Prayer Will Help

To write this it is making me cry
As I wonder why folk have to die?
My dearest mum and dad have been gone many years
But just to think of them brings on the tears.

I had such a wonderful father and mother too
Taught me the right things to do
When dear Dad was away in the war
Mum and I would stand at our front door.

She would say, 'Now Daddy, you and I are looking at the moon
God will keep him safe and bring him home soon.'
Mum taught me to say my prayers every night
Saying them still has guided me through life just right.

Now I thank God for my mum and dad
For a kind, loving life I have had
Now if you have lost someone and feel sad and low
Just give God a prayer, He will help you, I know.

Anne Churchward

A New Awakening

The time has come, for the angels to rejoice
When they hear the sound of Mother's sweet voice,
While we on Earth do weep and mourn
She will arise to meet the golden dawn.

St Peter's Gates will be opened wide
Whilst past loved ones await inside,
All life Mother had known, from this Earth before
Will be standing, to greet her at Heaven's door.

Laura Clarke

A Word

He loves to hate all men, her friends
No reason for his state
No intelligence to debate
Her vision is clear
Focusing thoughts

Their life together changed
Rearranged, separate
Now single her sight is clear
He disappears without a thought or tear
Her friends remain around
A lover is for a while
But a good friend is forever.

Learn to like, not love
Distance may divide
But you won't be hurt
As a lover will be devastated.

Kevin Clemo

Happy Times With Dad

Sports day and the fun
To win or lose a challenge
Right attitude of mind
Learie Constantine in Nelson 1930s
Cricket days with Dad
'Connie' was the man to watch
Delighted the crowds.

Mavis Catlow

A Letter To My Dad

Dear Dad
I am writing to say I love you
To say you'll always be on my mind
You were indeed a fine dad
We had many days of fun
I surely do miss you
I do wish you were still alive
I do wish you were still here
I do hope you're all right up there in Heaven
I know that God will look after you
I do believe that one day we will meet again
I do hope you are proud of me now
Me, David, your only son
I miss you for sure
I lost you when I was ten, back in 1972
You were indeed an excellently superb Dad
You were indeed the very, very best
Well dear Dad, I will always love you
You'll always be in my thoughts
Lots and lots of love always
Love your son
Love David.
XXXX

David J Hall

Sister She

At best she charismatic, sweet
At worst she still a double feat
Still enigmatic, artful, near
A born role model might she be dear.

Pure perfectionist is one
Amongst a host of assets, none
Of which are quite as great or grand
As just the way she'll lend a hand.

Clever, bright, smart; earnest too
She always set herself standard due
Her dedication, drive and deed
Her destiny knew that she'd succeed.

Kiranjit Kaur Rana

For My Father

With my father's genes
inside me, how can I believe
that the past is dead.
In pain, in joy, these are
his tears standing in my eyes.

He was small against the world's
indifference. Quietly
he went about his life,
and I allowed no space in mine
for him to blossom through.

He stood alone with his fire.
All that burned went
with him to the grave.
And now I wonder how I failed
to recognise his hunger.

Elsie Hamilton

My Dad

I was your firstborn, the beginning of three,
A new branch, to the family tree.
You loved me when I was just a babe,
Watched over me as I quietly laid.
As I grew older, and went to school,
You'd help me with homework, and play the fool.
Then I hit those teenage years,
Learnt of love lost, cried those broken-heart tears!
You'd stand by me through thick and thin,
Try to guide me, show patience when
I'd go out into the world, and make mistakes,
There you'd still be, ready to take
My pain away, and make life more,
Comfortable, it must have been a chore!
I'm now grown up, with my own family,
And through this experience, I can see,
A father's love and guidance, is life's special part,
Always to be treasured, deep in one's heart.
I love you Dad, you are simply the best!
You certainly pass that 'Best Dad' test!

Jennifer Collins

A Daughter

When she is born she is all snuggled up
You look at her, her skin is so soft
Her hair is so fine, you look at her
And say, 'Oh God, she is mine!'
When she is developing and she starts to smile
One tooth appears and there are tears for a while
But soon she is smiling and playing away
Then she is happy and cheerful as always at play.

Tess McHugh

Julian

A friendly face behind the counter
I always tried to catch his eye
Even though he was with a customer
He took time out to say hi.

Whenever he served me
We would exchange a joke or two
He was always very pleasant
And could not do enough for you.

When I read of his fatal accident
I remember the gentleman he was
So I have deep sorrow in his passing
And for his life we thank God.

So to you his friend or loved one
I offer my condolence to you
He will live in our memory
Our *Julian* we loved or knew.

L J Roche

God Bless You This Mother's Day

A prayer for Mother's Day that God up above
May bless you today with a heart full of love
That He'll send an angel to walk at your side
Matching your pace, guiding your every stride.

A prayer today that the sun warms your face
Wherever you wander, whatever the place
That bird sings sweetly, uplifting your heart
With Nature yet blessing all she'll impart.

A prayer that a rainbow with beautiful hue
Lends you its radiance, blessing you through
A prayer for no reason, but simply to bless
Making Mother's Day, a little bit special I guess.

Christopher R Slater

Olivia

You've got the sweetest little blossom
Lying in your arms
Waiting to beguile you
With her many charms.
But don't forget the wee boy
Who was first to fill your heart
Share the blossom with him
And they'll never want to part.

Daisy Adams

My Little Poppet Skye

The light of my life.
The joy of my being.
The greatest creation God ever invented.
Little nymph jumping from one to another
Feelings reaching to the very being
Love flowing, brimming over with glee
Giving pleasure to all those around her.
Waits for her presents
With open arms and eyes closed.
Such a feeling for life.
Learning all the time.
Growing in her sleep.
Vivid imagination!
Creating characters sometimes,
Living in a world of make-believe
Sleeping in the land of fairies and monsters.
My little poppet forever
Grow up with happiness for your grandma.

Joy Westmoreland

Clive

Dear little brown eyes
Come to me now,
Sweet little lips
Pursed up in a bow,
Darling wee arms thrown
Close round my neck,
Quick surge of love
'Gainst anxiety's trek,
Nothing to equal
That wee love of mine,
Bond of a mother
To child so divine;
Darling wee Clive
How grateful I am
To know that you're here
My sweet little lamb,
Whispering so low
As you call to me now
Words meant for Ashley
To relay on how
You'd like him to play with you
Ball kicked to 'Frou',
Chasing the rabbits,
Frightening the hens,
Quacking the ducks,
No solace he kens,
Mud piled on mud,
It's all in the game,
A white woolly poodle,
A little boy - Hame.

Valma June Streatfield

The Entranced Lovers

For centuries, Man acknowledged that
The phases of the Moon
And the notes of
Music bring out the best of all
Living things!

Farmers know when to plant crops,
That will yield an abundant harvest!
Fishermen know their largest
Catches and consequently,
Their greatest gains will happen
At the full Moon!
Even the seas themselves respond to the Moon
As it controls the rise of the tides!

With its remarkable ability to affect
The hearts and minds of individuals
At the same time,
The Moon and music have similar
Effect on our bodies and
Can harness the same power that
Affects the Earth and seas!

Just think, the same moon and music that has
Inspired the writings of
Poets and invited enchanted lovers
To walk hand in hand or
Dance cheek to cheek
Under its spellbinding
Light holds the power
To help change life forever!

Joana Efua Sam-Avor

For Sam And Becky

Watching them grow from the start,
Is something no money can buy,
Two children now in their teens,
School days will soon be a sigh.

I hope they'll be very happy,
In whatever they choose to do,
And keep the family together,
Yet see the world through eyes new.

At our age we do have the wisdom,
Help and advice is there,
I just hope we have a few days left,
To show them how much we care.

May they be as happy as we are,
Their mother and father too,
We thank them for so much pleasure,
Let's hope it continues through.

Ruth Wright

October Sun

You have come into my world
As the sun, the moon and stars
Casting hope from lonely shadows
Giving warmth inside my heart.

I knew that as I held you
My life would be complete
Those overwhelming moments
Now such a dark and distant dream.

Fear and trepidation
You so quickly washed away
To replace in me a loving, a longing
To enjoy our everyday.

Together as we are, peaceful, but never silent
Although you cannot speak
I know you understand me
That I will keep your life so sweet.

You are my little angel
A fair and pretty little queen
Together we will conquer
And achieve our every dream.

Bryony Freeman

The Young Musicians

There was a time when you played a merry tune
Joined by two big brothers in our living room

There was a time when you received three fairy dresses
Birthday presents all in pink, and you had a little think.

Quick as a wink, three party guests formed a line and did a dance,
Greeted by clapping hands and laughing delight from adults
                                                    helping out.

Many times you made me laugh, with your desire to make the very
                                                    best of life,
And not scream and shout when things didn't work out -
                                    quite the way you planned.

I smile when I think - baby it's you,
Now at the age of eight,
Samantha, to her grandparents, a precious gift for life.

Freda Grieve

My Grandson

A child's heart can spark and light,
The pathway on the darken night,
The love inside a heart so small
Could make me once again walk tall,
This little lad, how could he know
That he had made my heart aglow,
Sadness faded, skies came blue
My life; this lad had made it new,
With words, 'I love you being here with me,'
Made his grandad's heart as big as three.

V N King

Baby It's You!

Oh baby it's you, making shining our view!
Symbol unique of everything new.
God's blessing, parents freely confessing,
Changing their lives forever, praying mostly
For good health, whilst a bonus
Would be a bonny baby clever.
Binding a family together in foul and fair weather,
Glorious promise of the future to come,
To pride, impossible not to succumb.
Gaze on a soundly sleeping tot,
Secure a memory never to be forgot,
Burned into the brain and there firmly remain,
Beautiful picture to be revisited again and again.
Whilst still in the pram, parents will begin to plan
Though life is a lottery, wish
Their infant to grab the jackpot!
Naturally, life may not be a happy lot
But to ensure and secure a golden future,
Mum and Dad will give it all they've got.
At the end of the road, we'll turn around and say,
'Oh baby, it's you who made our day.'

Graham Watkins

Poem For Little Liam

Liam is smiling, Liam is laughing,
Liam is looking a picture of joy,
Everything's fine in his world at the moment,
Bright as a lark is this slap-happy boy.
Snuggling and bouncing at sister and brother,
Isn't he lucky to have them around?
Grasping their fingers with loving approval,
Longing to get his feet on the ground.
May you grow up, my gorgeous great-grandson,
Happy with what this life has in store,
May the stars shine for you, may the birds sing for you,
Life's an adventure and never a bore.
Little Liam, may you be merry,
Have all the things I'm wishing for you,
I shall be gone but others will love you,
Little Liam, may your dreams all come true.

Margaret Rose Harris

My Loved Ones

A beautiful angel, a baby so sweet
From the hair on her head, and the toes on her feet
A smile, a laugh, just a bundle of fun
Her eyes always shine, like a summer's day sun
This wonderful child, a glory to behold
Wrapped up in a blanket, away from the cold
Each little child is our future, you see
Our children, their children, our family tree
Every child precious, their life's in our arms
Hide them from hurt and life's terrible harms
My daughter, her daughter, these sweet girls, my life
Nickola, Talisha and my darling wife
Daughter and granddaughter, precious to me
I write in this poem, so the whole world can see
I promise to look after you, and be your life's tutor
A child's still a child, whatever the future
So God bless all children, no matter what, when or where
Just call on your mum and dad and see we will be there

Carl Fricker

Apple Of Their Eye

Rock-a-by baby,
Lay down your sweet head
On the soft pillow
In your downy bed.

All the gold in the world
Would not buy you.
Around their heart curled
Child only just on view.

A present from Heaven,
May love surround you.
Sweet dreams pretty babe,
Baby days are few.

Granny and Grandad
Are so very proud
And they would choose you
Out of any crowd.

Rock-a-by baby,
Flickering smiles seen.
Can you remember
Or are you having a dream?

May your life be long,
Good, happy and true,
Whatever one wishes
For a baby so new.

J Millington

Adoption's The Option

Giving birth was never meant to be
For Dad and me.
We waited what seemed a lifetime
But that joy was not to be mine.
Until the day you were brought to us
Without ceremony or fuss.
A lovely boy, two years old,
Big blue eyes, hair of gold.
Chubby body, cheeky smile,
It didn't matter we'd had to wait a while.
This was our boy we had waited for,
No hesitation, who could ask for more?
Always lively, good at school,
No problems growing up, but nobody's fool.
He took all the knocks of growing up,
Generosity and kindness was part of his make-up.
Now that Dad and I are getting older,
He's taken it upon his shoulder
To look after us as much as he can,
Which makes him a very great man.
In our eyes, nothing's too much trouble,
So nothing can burst our bubble
About our boy, 'Peter' by name,
Adoption's the name of our game.

Hazel J Palmer

My Son Got Married Last Week!

My son got married last week!
I love to hear those words.
I am a bit of a bore
Telling everyone I meet.

My son got married last week!
I have a smile all over my face.
The looks they give each other
Make the world a better place.

My son got married last week!
'Change the record,' someone says.
I will when I hear the news
Of the patter of tiny feet!

Margaret Rowe

In Remembrance Of Mum And Dad

'Cut the mattress up and sew me inside it,' my late brother Terry said.
He got a good hiding, while I slid under the bed.
Someone made us two wooden daggers,
While playing Indians and cowboys, we stabbed the leather suite.
Did we get a really good hiding? We knew when we were beat.
We were two little terrors and deserved every hiding we got,
Though I can laugh about the memories, tears we shed quite a lot.
She was still a wonderful mother, to me she was one of the best,
Now she is in God's garden, taking a well-earned rest.
One day I hope to be reunited with my mother, and also my dad,
No one knows what life holds for them as we learn new skills
                                                      without strife,
But I'm really glad that my mother and dad got together
And led such a wonderful life.

James Ayrey

Loved Ones

When I first met my husband and stepdaughter, Louise,
I was lost, ill, cold and full of spite.
I thought I'd have no chance
To turn the wrong to right,
The love we now share together
Through good and bad,
Through every kind of weather.
Picnics, walks in the woods, zoos and beautiful things,
The simple ways,
I never thought I'd have another sunny day
And now I'm full of love
For I now know there's a God above.
For Steve and Louise, they make me feel pleased.
I love them both and will always be with them
For they are my loved ones.

Rosalind Ann Webb

Maltese Baby

I sometimes feel a child at heart
Surrounded by my special toys
Of model cars and teddy bears
(Lying on the tops of shelves.)

In albums stacked beside my bed
Are photographs of faltering steps,
Beaming with my golden curls,
Dancing 'mongst the Dartmoor lambs.

There are many more preserved in time,
(Schooldays, Ghana, Essex fields),
The Sixties and those teenage pains,
Rebellion in a restless mood.

Through fifty years of growing up,
My mother has been there for me.
I do believe I'm still her babe,
Arriving on that New Year's Day.

She has been so very proud,
Supporting goals I have achieved,
From shyness to some closest friends,
Encouraging each new idea.

The road's been long from counting toes
And gurgling in my Maltese pram,
For I've become a happy man,
Born again - my Norfolk world.

Steve Glason

The First Grandchild

Dearest babe so small, loved by all, your parents' pride and joy
The wondrous gift God gave to us, a beautiful baby boy
So snug and adorable, you are truly our delight
We care for you continually because you are a sensation never out
                                                                          of our sight

This dearest little bundle who receives such loving care
We enjoy every moment, such a wonder to compare
On occasions there is a whimper, immediately we are on the alert
Either to be fed or changed, from our duties we never shirk

Many said you are bound to be spoiled, we retort, 'Why not?'
As many gather to view and exclaim all around your cot
Grandparents give of their good advice and are so eager to please
They also assist in the management, we appreciate deeds
Continually watching over you, there is never a doubt
As you progress in wonderment, we let those woeful wishes out
From such a tiny baby your progress is maintained
As you gaze at us with beautiful blue eyes and a smile, we are amazed

Blessed little fellow now responding to our voice
Sleeping like a cherub in silence I rejoice
Observing those infant movements we are surprised and amazed
Upon waking you play and gurgle and understand our ways
We thank the Lord continually as blessed with this bundle of joy
Who now has made our lives complete and he never does annoy
Grandparents are also proud as they spoil our infant son
They say it is their privilege, he the wondrous gift, our number one.

R D Hiscoke

Nature's Gift
(Dedicated to my baby grandson, Miles Hugh)

The long-awaited babe is here,
His small perfection oh so dear,
All the stresses of this earth,
Eclipsed by the wonder of his birth.

Day by day we will behold
Mysteries of new life unfold.
No other miracle can compare,
This awe and wonder is so rare.

Mavis Johnson

Our Firstborn

Baby, baby, baby,
Oh how the years have flown
Since in that little white bundle
We brought you, our firstborn, home
It has been with pride we've watched you grow
All your firsts recorded in my head
Never tiring of watching
As you lay sleeping in your bed
We watched you through your teen years
And off to uni far from home
Always welcoming the news
Of work and pleasures as it came
Now you are a dad with grown-up girls
And I am alone since your dad passed on
But in my solace I still see
The pictures of my firstborn baby son.

Daphne Fryer

Baby Love

It's quite conclusive, without any doubt,
I'm carrying a child inside, not out!
I'm so excited, can't wait to tell,
We've waited so long and been through Hell.
Month after month, hoping and praying
But the look on my face went without saying.
We'd given up hope of having a child,
The thought of 'never' drove me wild.
Now at last our dream's come true,
Shall I buy pink or baby blue?
To have this life growing inside,
It's a 'wonder' of nature, it can't be denied.

A A Trick

Beau - My Great Grandson

I look upon the face of God
When I gaze upon this face of love
This cherub child, sent from above
Content and happy in his play
His laughing soul out on display
His sunny smile, deep disposition
No greater joy or sweet transition
Spreads upon this soul of mine
To see this tiny face a-shine
Yet onward through this world to go
This 'innocence' born of love.
Named Beau.

Hazel Brydon

A Tiny Baby

A tiny baby cries in turning space
And watches Earth learning its easy pace
A guardian angle she spies, then giggles
With fingers and toes that point and wiggle

Is there an angel resting by my side?
Or perched like a parrot, wings out wide
On shoulders ancient mine carry her
Like a kitten I hear the angel purr

So does our God a tickling stick possess?
To tickle ribs and toes, any recess
He has a sense of fun I have no doubt
But look when the Devil wins, does he pout?

Now my guardian swings along
And whistles tunes among the happy throng
In cool of the evening she sits on my bed
And keeps away monsters, the evil dead

As morning skies now clear she watches
The city just rises yawning loud washes
I thank the Lord in a simple prayer soft
For guardian angel's now gone aloft

O blue the seas are burning fields of love
And red the blood is falling from above
A rook is crying under arches of cloud
A prayer goes up and God is highly proud.

David Sheasby

Another Generation

I held her in my arms,
This tiny mystery,
I held her, fed her, cared for her,
Loved and nurtured my baby daughter.

I walked her, talked to her, trained her,
This tiny mystery,
Then one day she spoke to me,
She touched and recognised me.

I took her to school,
Nursed her through all ills,
I cried for her, shared joys and sorrows with her,
This growing mystery.

Attended her degree day,
So proud of my baby daughter,
She left me - her fortune to seek,
Introduced her beau to me,
Rang me on engagement day.

I waited at the church for her,
My darling little girl,
This cloud of tulle moved up the aisle,
I saw her wed the one she loved.

Today, I held her in my arms again,
This tiny mystery,
I welcomed another generation,
My baby's baby daughter.

Janet Cavill

My Girl

When I think of my girl, my thoughts are always happy,
Always kind to me and never, ever snappy.
The day she went away was the saddest of my life,
I felt as if my heart had been cut out by a knife.
Through the years, her absence I accept,
But many times I've just sat down and wept.
The telephone is now my friend,
Our conversations never end.
Always cheerful, merry and bright,
She makes my heart feel everything's right.
When she comes home to see me,
I thank my God on bended knee.
When she goes back again,
I feel a never-ending pain.
Would not change my Jacquie in any single way,
Just to hear her voice really makes my day.
Though she's many miles from me,
It seems she's here and will forever be.
She is my darling daughter,
This wonderful fact will never alter,
I thank God that I'm her mum,
Her very being is like the sun.

Olive Young

Curtis, Aged Seven

Like your big brother I was at your birth,
Mummy pushed for all her worth,
Out you came, squalling and bawling,
It did not seem long before you were crawling.
Your eyes were so large and very deep brown,
But on your face you wore a frown.

Food did not seem to matter to you,
But all was well as you grew and grew.
Mummy and Daddy got Pepper, the dog,
When you visited us, you would find a frog,
By looking for ages into our pond,
When stones went in, you would abscond!

Curtis, you have grown into a loving boy,
To see you is a constant joy.
You always want to come and stay,
One at a time is what I say.
But you always bring your friend Turtle,
Together down the garden you do hurtle.

We took you to our village pantomime,
You overcame your shyness just in time,
You went on stage, your shyness melted away,
As you sang, 'If you go down in the woods today.'
Granddad and I felt that you deserved the prize.
'I did it,' you said; we had tears in our eyes.

Kathy Johnson

A Bond Of Love

Tiny fingers, little pink toes,
A soft wisp of hair and a tiny button nose.
As I silently watch over her as she peacefully sleeps,
This is a memory I'll always keep.
Then as I watch her grow year after year,
There will be days of happiness, laughter and tears.
But whatever the future holds I'll enjoy these days of bliss,
For these special moments are too precious to miss.
So when two little arms are held out to me,
And a soft tiny voice calls out, 'Mummy, Mummy,'
I'll take her in my arms, my heart bursting with pride,
Knowing that bond of love has been realised,
As no treasures on Earth could ever compare
With this gift of love, my beautiful baby daughter.

Kathleen Webb

Her First Snowman

Her first time to see the snow fly,
Flicker, flutter about - then fall,
To see how snowdrifts can rise high,
While sheer whiteness can cover all.

A first time to build a snowman,
To watch him as he grows and grows.
With gloved hands, pile on all she can,
Now and then stamp to warm up toes.

She may stop to make a snowball,
Perhaps the first she's ever made.
A quick throw may just hit the wall.
Of those thrown back, she's not afraid.

Though gloves are wet after the fight,
There's still the snowman to finish.
He needs a head before it's night.
A hat on top of that her wish.

A carrot makes a splendid nose,
Two pebbles give him two black eyes.
Jolene needs to warm hands and toes -
But she's helped a giant to rise . . .

At that first time to see snow fly,
Flicker, flutter about and fall,
To dig through where snowdrifts lie,
So there's a *snowman* by the wall!

C M Creedon

Unfathered In The Packed Street
(To my as much loved father as time's life and thereafter)

The heart-tearing wave of blood sweeping through
The place blurred the curtain of avid vision.
And the traumatised brain conceded
An unwilling procrastination of this woe's account.
The breath-gnawing stealer struck
The sandy stage of life.
And the vacant eyes stared at the vacuum
Left by *his* abrupt absence in the swarming street.
A few words were strangulated
In an unsounded shadowy sepulchre of silence,
In the melancholic mire of heart, unsaid, unheard.
While the light deserted the dark dungeon
Yet again to be on an infinite furlough,
But the loyal breath lingered till
Lastly parting the company.
And the deafening cogency of
His words surpassed all shutters,
'Life surrendered walking in the street
Is much better than the one setting in the bed.'
While somewhere on the extant side of the split
A few soundless thoughts stirred, surged, soared
And then sank in an incommunicable inner dark.

Rizwan Saeed Ahmed

Anniversary Sonnet For My Father
(Dedicated with much love to Dad who passed away 14/8/78: heart attack)

From time's ultimate beginning
To time's ultimate end: with fabulous
Angels and darkness where glorious
Night talks to me of its winning
Of beauty and wonder: I gasp brimming
Spiritual as I gaze wondrous
Into the depths of its enormous
Solitude: billions of stars spinning
Billions of planets beyond belief:
This staggering world God made to look
So simple unbearably in relief:
So beautifully written His holy book,
Beyond comprehension of human mind,
In awe spiritual love of human kind.

Edmund Saint George Mooney

At Seventy-Two

At seventy-two I bought my first CD.
What does it matter? Who cares?
I care. I cry . . . my sons can play what they will:
For them to touch a button and call forth
The music of the centuries and of all the world
Is just . . . normal.

But for me . . . well, I remember my father.
In the thirties, he bought the family a gramophone.
Wax records, extracts of opera - how did he know those?
Old needles - later used by me as shells in the toy guns we had
In the *second* war to end all wars.

I learnt from him, not from his words, but from
The love his actions showed. My love of music
Now still but half-formed, came from him.
In his life, hurt by the agonies of rheumatism,
He did his best. He carried on: he loved my mother

And my sister knew he loved us both. He was
The conductor of the music in our lives;
And so I cry for him, for his hard, long life,
And his scarcely, rarely spoken love for us all:
So now, because of him, I can buy a CD.
And with love, I can cry.

Geoffrey Speechly

Dear Dad

It's been a while since you went away
And I have made many mistakes
Each day I think about you
How you struggled through
Working hard to be you
With lots of sadness inside
To lose your love is heartbreaking
And to find a place deep in your heart
To place them
Many sit like medals in my heart
But Dad, you have the biggest part
Because you'll always be the gold
That I treasure
So like this feather
I know you're near
And I wipe my tears
Wish you were here

Linda Bevan

The Last Post
(For my dad, Terry Fuller, 28th July 1942 - 20th May 2007, who chose a beautiful morning to enter eternity)

A clear blue sky
With a soft, gentle breeze -
An empty garden
With tall, majestic trees.
I feel your touch
But you are not there -
You are free of pain
And without a care,
The world will be empty without you
To talk and to share,
Thoughts and visions
Of life day-to-day.
The Last Post is playing,
Calling you home.
You were the best dad anyone could wish for;
The only one.

Debbie Nobbs

Being A Dad (This Is Totally True)

I love being a dad,
it was the best Christmas present I ever had!
I never thought I ever would . . .
because in movies/books: *'Disabled can't - and never should.'*

It started in 1995 when we went to Rome,
my ex and her children went into a shop to buy honeycomb!
A nun went by and blessed me,
nine months later, Hannah was born, at 12.03.

Now she is growing up, I just love the hugs . . .
occasionally you do need the earplugs!
Or it is, 'Dad, can I have more money?
I have been good, and it is sunny.'

First it was Janette's children of two,
my stepchildren, twins - Daniel and Lou.
Then came lovely Hannah, and I wanted to yell . . .
Next came my godson . . . Darnell!

Hopefully Hannah will give me grandchildren one day . . .
maybe we could all go out and play!

Barry Ryan

A Poem For Dad

I'll be forever grateful for each day you gave me,
You've been my inspiration,
My world is a better place because of you.
You saw the best there was in me
And always gave me hope.
You showed me the way to the right path
And I will always remember you're my dad
And no one can take your place.

Alexis Jarrett

Too Proud

When my dad was a little lad
He loved to ride a horse
He got his chance as stable lad
Coming first on Ripon's course
He rode so many times and won
His head grew out of size
My dad so proud, he knew it all
But he wasn't very wise
The big day came, the trainer said
'Now trot down to the post'
But my dad had different plans
He galloped off at speed to boast
He couldn't stop when to the start he came
Passing horses at the gate
He galloped on and out of sight
But the others couldn't wait
When at last my dad pulled up
What a shock as the field advanced
He leapt off and ran away
And left the horse to take its chance

Catherine Armstrong

Things My Father Taught Me

When autumn came my dad came home
The war was on, the food was scarce
Walking we did go, edible fungi hunting
We knew poisonous toadstools,
Impressing as we walked
Never touch such beautiful earthstar,
Death cap or red fly agaric
Edible ink caps, chanterelle puffballs,
Delicious field ones too
Wood blewit, the best of all,
Oyster mushrooms, fantastic
Dad, to me you were Father Nature,
The best dad of all.

To the blast in Seaham on your bike for coal
We never starved or ever were cold,
The time you were home
The merchant navy, the secret service,
Torpedoed thrice
Animals loved you, how many oil-slicked birds
You've saved?
Cat and dog named Rags and Bones,
Canary, Dick, humour too
Dad I have carried on nearly seventy-two
Learning from you.
To put myself in Gilligan's place,
Artist and sculptor I am
Writing as well, thanks to you and Mam
(Another story)
Have remembered if I have two of something
Give one away
Then the one I have left disintegrates
Was that the best advice?
I think so, you never swore or smacked,
Or broke your marriage vows
Old Joseph Ritchie, I loved you, the best dad of all.

Iris Williams

My Family

My family are farming folk
Who work hard for a living,
Survived the great depression
But always to be saving.

We are gentle country people
With a love of simple things,
Of wildlife and nature
That things in season brings.

They were ordinary farmers
Happy with their station
With no pretence of grandeur
Empty pride or affection.

A much respected family
Straight in business dealing
Attending market weekly
For buying and selling

We went to church on Sundays
In a special pew to sit,
And for the brass collection plate
A shiny silver threepenny bit.

Ellen Lock

My Lovely Dad

When I was a child he gave everything for me,
He loved me.
When I fell down he picked me up again,
If I called for him he came.
When I cried he dried my tears,
When I was scared he calmed my fears.
We laughed together and cried together,
At times we even fought together.
I was so proud to say he was my father -
I hope he was proud of me too.
He was my dad
And I loved him.

Kim Thompson

My Dear Dad

There's a hole in my heart where you've been o'er the years;
There's a well which has dried with the shedding of tears;
There's a gap and a void which I know can't be filled'
There's a cry in the night which will not be stilled;
There's an ache, how it hurts, when I think of your pain,
And the knowledge, dear Dad, that we can't talk again.

There's anguish, dear Dad, for your hurt and your sorrow.
Such sadness for me, when for you, no tomorrow.
When I know you have left on your journey afar,
When I wonder if ever I'll find the bright star,
That has guided and helped me from birth 'til today,
When you left me, dear Dad, and you just went away.

You left with such speed, with no time for goodbyes,
But I saw the great sadness in the blue of your eyes.
For you wanted to stay, still so much to do.
Oh how can I manage, dear Dad, without you?
There'll be comfort in the memories, that will never depart,
Of the times we spent together buried deep within my heart.

You showed me how you loved me, showed me daily that you cared,
And I'm grateful for the good times and the laughter which we shared.
Of all the men who ever lived, I'm so glad you were my dad,
For me the very best of pals that I could ever have.
You'll stay with me forever, Dad, and you'll always play a part,
Within my life, my whole life through, locked safely in my heart.

Patricia Marland

My Dad

My dad worked hard all his working life,
He had a good sense of humour and a gift to tell stories.
When young he played practical jokes on some friends.
He loved shooting, walking, fishing, golf and birdwatching
And encouraged his children in these sports.
He loved his spaniels and other dogs,
He kept throughout his married life.
He wrote a book about his work.
He loved Switzerland and other beautiful old places
Where he and my mother led groups of people on holiday
For fifty years - during the war the holidays were in England.
He loved and served God leading Crusader classes.
He was a reader in the Anglican church and a lay preacher
                                                        in the Methodist.
He took services in churches and chapels.
When older, God took him to his eternal home,
Now united with my mother.
I thank the Lord for my father and his love for his family.

Jean Martin-Doyle

To My Father

Today you're like teddy-one-ear
in your brown sweater
with the black diamond markings
torn where it caught on the side-car mudguard.
You're safe as a deposit box
sharing the day. She
in cotton mill buildings,
their rubber corridors stagnant
with patients' dinners,
collects her soul.

Today we are getting acquainted.
You are not as she said.
I hear you say, 'That's the way.
That was a silly thing to do.
How can we sort it out?'
At the unexpected phone call,
'Run along, enjoy yourself!'
I put on the orange shift dress I made,
cut out, ready to sew from Woman's Realm.
When I go, you don't complain.

Returning I'm bowled over
(finding you still in the garage
tuning the carburettor)
at how your isolation stings me.

Rosemary Benzing

I Never Had A Dad

I never had a dad
Who really cared for me.
Mine never hugged or kissed me
Or sat me on his knee.

He never took me for a walk,
Or tucked me up in bed.
He never put his arm round me
Or patted on my head.

He never helped me clean my teeth
Or taught me to tie laces.
He never tried to make me laugh
By pulling funny faces.

He never helped us play with toys
Or have games upon the beach.
He never visited our school
To see what teachers teach.

I used to hear my friends all say
What they did with their dad
And I could never understand
Why my dad was so bad.

He was just a master figure
Who came and passed us by
Who ate and slept amongst us
And never said 'goodbye'.

Helen E Langstone

Roundabout Of Life

With walking stick and silver hair
Dozing in a comfy chair
As a child, he'd listen to you
Special things he did for you
Shared with him, soon were shed
All the worries in your head
Years have flown, quickly too
Whatever happened to 'little you'?
Roles reverse, wait and see
Give back all, love's not free!
It's your turn to give back all
As Dad did when you were small.

Now Dad has worries in his head,
But told to you, soon are shed
As off he goes to his warm bed
With these worries off his chest
Like you once, he now can rest
Years go by and we find out
Life is like a roundabout
Now that Dad is eighty-two
Give back the love he gave to you.

Sitting in his comfy chair
Sunlight dancing on silver hair
Years of love, care and strife
On the roundabout of life
We all to old age are bound
And as the years turn around
The roundabout of destiny's found.

Sheila Walters

Daddy Observed

I often go to the window
To watch Daddy go by.
The dogs and he are a trilogy
Of love, trust and respect.
Large and small walking tall,
Ten legs stepping out happily
Make a delightful prospect.

In the rain, with his cap on straight,
Daddy will never accelerate.
The pace is geared to the shortest legs.
Westie's companion never begs
For longer strides or slacker leads.
All three are content. Daddy proceeds
Whatever the weather, even when he needs an umbrella.
Twice he improvised when it was fair;
First a bicycle, then a pushchair!
But always the dogs, trotting side by side.
The baby had a privileged ride.

I don't speak to Daddy, so there is no way
I can tell him that his trio always makes my day.

I wonder whose Daddy he is.

Louie Carr

Father

He took me by the hand, led me laughing
in May woods
along green ways
we walked shores together
paddled in seas
in summer's days

He reached up, gathered stars from sky
made me a bracelet
on a silver wire
misty tears are diamonds
their radiance
was suddenly afire

He stopped, gathering flowers on path
held out fairest
as a gift to me
he took a bird from sky
telling it to sing
me a melody

Death took his heart, pulled
his shape awry, I saw the
look on his face
as he fell at my feet
memories remain here inside
this palace of gardens.

Teresa Webster

The Daddy Dance

When God the Father came to me,
In drunken stupor I came in,
A veteran of this world's great war,
A winner on the side of sin.

He spoke to me of things not seen
Through eyes glazed over, shadow dim.
The truth revealed, the veil removed,
I saw my soul's true worth to Him.

And then He took me in His arms,
And danced, so gentle, full of grace,
A Father's love for a child's return,
I rested in His sweet embrace.

And as my Father held me then,
My children's father, here on Earth,
Has held them safely through the night;
Was there to see each through their birth.

He danced with them when they were young,
A dance so gentle, full of grace;
And though exhausted from the day,
Found time for each bedtime embrace.

He is a man of strength and faith,
A somber man at one's first glance;
But underneath that serious guise,
Are memories of 'the Daddy dance'.

Joy Kelly

The Legend Of The Heroes

Heroes come and then they fall,
They stand in many forms.
They leave the trail of legacy
Just like summer storms.

Some stand firm in defiance
Against all prejudice and chance.
Others just pass a kind word,
A kiss, a smile, a dance.

Knights of shining armour,
Or poets of pleasing verse.
Actors who can charm a crowd,
A footballer? Or worse?

Could it be some mentor?
Or maybe just a teacher?
Is your hero a high goddess?
Or maybe just a preacher?

Some are deadly in battle
And some make peace not war.
Others wear a uniformed strip
And hit the net, they score.

Some heroes' names echo down
Right through the halls of time.
Others may be forgot about
Before you've read this rhyme.

Some heroes fight for the people,
Others calm a maddening crowd.
Knelt in reverend and silent prayer
Or battles cry out loud.

Of all my heroes perched at the top
Is a man who stands out tall!
He's been there from the start,
My father, best of all.

Stuart Adams

My Dad - Captain Of Love

In our childhood firm rule kept life orderly each day.
Dad; the master of the house, Mum came next we'd say.
Then according to our ages we were next in line.
Most likely was the same in your house, as it was in mine.
Each morning when we wakened, Dad was not at home.
He had gone to asphalt roads, cycling on his own.
No staff transport, was *your* job to be there by start time.
If your dad worked far from home, he got there same as mine.
So men could use asphalt, pots must be lit at 5am each day.
You needed to be up at two to cycle all that way.
He had to take a box of food so he'd not hungry be.
No coffee shops, but pricey cafés served by smart 'nippy'.
He could not afford that each day, so waited until night
To have his cooked meal. Tasty stew alright?
We kids talked about our day, telling what we'd done.
He would say he couldn't eat the last two bits of bun.
We would beam as he patiently gave bit to brother and bit to me.
Each evening was my job to go to paper shop,
Fetch shilling tin of Walters fags. Tomorrow he'd smoke that lot.
If we'd behaved and helped our mum, Dad sometimes gave to both.
A halfpenny to get some sweets, we tried not to be a sloth.
He went to British Legion with Mum every Saturday.
While we played on swings in park opposite we'd sway.
If naughty he never hit us, we were sent to bed without out tea.
Him knowing full well Mum would sneak up some for free.
He'd lie on sand watching us play on Bournemouth beach.
He'd lost sight of one eye but we reckoned that,
He could see better with that one than any dog or cat.
Looking back on all those years, only one regret I have.
I would have liked a lot more years with mine, the best of dads.

Barbara Goode

Thank You Mum

Thanks Mum for lovingly caring for me
All through my childhood
Cooking, cleaning, washing and shopping
Comforting me when I was sad
Telling me not to be afraid, but to trust in God
Who freely gives us all things
And telling me of Jesus who came to save me
Sharing with me a prayer of forgiveness
When I first gave my life to Him
Making sure I was smartly dressed for school
With enough money for dinner
For holidays with Dad and my brother
With the excitement of adventure
Taking me to places I had never seen
With beautiful landscapes, rivers and lakes
Laughing as I swam in the sea
And enjoying animals on a farm or in a zoo
Or praying for me when I left home
Inspiring me to care for others
And strengthening them in their faith in the Lord
Now your work has been done
And you rest in Heaven with all the saints
Who the victory have won
And look down on me as I travel this earthly road
Until I see you again in Heaven
I'll always remember you with affection
And hope to share the faith and love you had
With others whose lives are struggling
In life's stormy seas.

David Cooke

Where Have You Gone?

Where have you gone? oh Dad my love
To soar the heights of Heaven's love
He's not afraid and he does not fear
He knows that God is ever near
Just touch His arms, He'll embrace you now
I know, I feel it inside somehow.

The sense of peace, but a loss I'll miss
I love you now, I gently kiss
I speak this high up above -
How I will miss you, oh my love.

Months ago, we did talk and speak
Of past regrets, of things I'll keep
And the joys and memories of laughters shared
I am one with you now, oh how I care.

I turn to you, to share my love
To say it gently to your face, I love you
As I now embrace.

I whisper to you up above
Goodbye for now, you'll not be long
In my heart you do belong.

Go to where the angels sing
You'll be at peace on Heaven's wing.

Thésie Jenkinson

Forward Press Information

We hope you have enjoyed reading this book - and that you will continue to enjoy it in the coming years.

If you like reading and writing poetry drop us a line, or give us a call, and we'll send you a free information pack.

Alternatively if you would like to order further copies of this book or any of our other titles, then please give us a call or log onto our website at
www.forwardpress.co.uk

Forward Press Ltd. Information
Remus House
Coltsfoot Drive
Peterborough
PE2 9JX
(01733) 890099